MAY 1 3 2010

P9-DDV-340

Armitage's
Vines and Climbers

A GARDENER'S GUIDE
TO THE BEST VERTICAL PLANTS

ALLAN M. ARMITAGE

TIMBER PRESS
Portland · London

Frontispiece: *Clematis* 'Durandii' weaving through
Schizophragma integrifolium
Opposite: *Canavalia gladiata* seeds in a pod

Many thanks to all my plant friends who contributed images to
supplement mine: Suzy Bales, Dan Benarcik, Robert Bowden,
Lyndy Broder, Donnie Carlson, Meg Green, Lane Greer, Loren
Hallstrom, Judy Laushman, Alan Shapiro, Vincent Simeone,
Ben Walcott, Richard Warren, Susan Watkins, Tim Wood, and
Jonathan Wright; to Judy Laushman, whose keen eyes looked over
every word; and to my lifelong editor, Frances Farrell, whose skills
always make my writing better. — AMA

Photographs are by the author unless otherwise noted.

Published in 2010 by Timber Press, Inc.

The Haseltine Building
133 S.W. Second Avenue, Suite 450
Portland, Oregon 97204-3527
www.timberpress.com

2 The Quadrant
135 Salusbury Road
London NW6 6RJ
www.timberpress.co.uk

Text designed by Susan Applegate
Printed in China

Library of Congress Cataloging-in-Publication Data

Armitage, A. M. (Allan M.)
    Armitage's vines and climbers/Allan M. Armitage.—1st ed.
      p. cm.
    Includes indexes.
    ISBN 978-1-60469-039-2
    1. Ornamental climbing plants—United States—Handbooks,
manuals, etc. 2. Ornamental climbing plants—Canada—Handbooks, manuals, etc. 3. Climbing plants—United States—Handbooks, manuals, etc. 4. Climbing plants—Canada—Handbooks,
manuals, etc. I. Title. II. Title: Vines and climbers.
    SB427.A75 2010
    635.9'74—dc22   2009032437

A catalog record for this book is also available
from the British Library.

To Laura, Heather, and Jonathan

When a child is born,
you have no idea what parenting is about,
and you hope to do a few things right.
Our children make us look brilliant;
every day they make us proud.

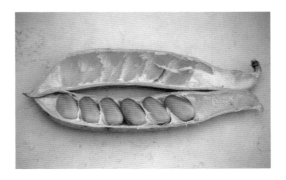

Rosa 'American Pillar'
at Longwood Gardens

Contents

Introduction
9

A-to-Z Vines
13

Lists of Vines with Specific Characteristics and Uses
205

Useful Conversions
208

Index of Botanical Names
209

Index of Common Names
211

Canavalia gladiata, fruit

Introduction

IT IS SPRING in north Georgia. Dogwoods, redbuds, wisteria, and jasmine combine with finches, cardinals, and titmice on a day I wish I could bottle up to savor during the heat of August. I am sitting here on the raised wooden deck at home, minding my own business, sipping a little red wine, and thinking about nothing . . .

Then I look down at the deck. I can't help but notice half a dozen stems of my climbing rose poking their way up through the slats, gasping for light. I have a vision of some creepy sci-fi movie (*Revenge of the Vines?*), and my incredibly quick brain thinks, "What are they doing there?"

I have been experimenting with annual and perennial vines and climbers for many years, and whenever I "discover" some crazy new rambler, I wonder why they are not better known. I quickly realize that people who want vines in their garden are often stymied by the lack of choice in retail centers. Boston ivy, English ivy, climbing roses, and the ubiquitous clematis are often the only options, relegating all the other wonderful choices to mail order and seed packets. And then there are those people who look at English ivy and wisteria in the woods and immediately equate all vines with the word "invasive."

Another vine book
There are dozens of books about vines—but not too many in the last ten years, and even fewer by North American authors (seems the English and the Irish are the undisputed vine experts—maybe it is those 500-year-old rock walls that were always in need of covering). Many of the vine books out there are undeniably comprehensive and colorful, but they all seem to be missing something. The gardener in me asked, "But what about the killing frosts, the sapping humidity, the howling winds, or the long hot summers in many parts

of this continent?" So, I looked around for what I could find and filled my gardens with as many of these crazy climbers as I could. And then I traveled wherever possible to see and learn about what I couldn't find. The more I saw, the more I realized that maybe I had something to say about this group of plants tucked into nooks and crannies by hundreds of gardeners around North America. I traveled, I gardened, and I learned, and I have included the good, the bad, the ugly, and the invasive. My budget ran out long before my curiosity.

Annual vs perennial vines

Gardeners always ask if a plant is perennial, as if having an annual in the garden was a cardinal sin. My short answer—"Who cares?" I understand that people crave perenniality in their gardens, and promoting annual vines may not be a particularly logical choice for the retail garden shop. However, if we're true gardeners, we should try to appreciate the weird and the wonderful, and if we can get only a season's worth of wonderful blooms from them before the cold takes them out, big deal. If you haven't tried hyacinth bean (*Lablab purpureus*) or a butterfly vine (*Mascagnia*), don't dismiss annual vines quite yet. I love them all, annual or perennial, and quickly discovered I will never discover them all.

Vines are not for everybody

I am a gardener and a plant nut. I am also old and rickety—and getting more so with time—so I think twice about using demanding, high-maintenance plants. Ripping out impolite vines that have overstayed their welcome or brought their entire family with them does nothing for me. Others, even those a little younger than I, say the same thing, and warn of the heartaches of Chinese wisteria, English ivy, bittersweet, Virginia creeper, and trumpet vine. It seems that vines have more than their fair share of invasive members, and we need to be aware of them. That being said, my best advice? Choose your plants thinking about what it will look like in five years, and don't close your mind. Painting all vines with the wisteria brush isn't fair to the many wonderful little-known vines that don't have any intention of eating the house. Perhaps that's why I believe annual vines have such a rich future. I can have my moonflowers, Spanish flag, and sweet peas without any worry of a sore back.

What is included

I suppose I should include all those neat line drawings showing different trellis systems or climbing posts, or how to dig a hole; however, if you don't know how to dig a hole, you shouldn't be reading this book. As far as trellis systems are concerned, I am too poor or too confused by the choices. I simply find a fence, an arbor, or even a tree, help the vines when young, and then get out of the way. If they are spectacular, I take full credit; if they are puny, I blame the trellis. Discovering what will climb up that fence, trellis, or tree is far more fun than digging fence post holes. The "what it is" part of the book is my attempt to suggest why anybody would even choose a particular plant, and if so, how you could explain to your troubled neighbor why it is eating his roof. Yes, I have included plants that the more militant wing of native plant groups will be upset about. "If it is invasive, why tell people about it?" I included them because they are not invasive in many parts of the country, they are being sold in nurseries, and ignoring them loses an opportunity to tell people of their potential aggressiveness. Not including English ivy in a vine book is like not including the Edsel in an automotive history book.

I included propagation, etymology, and identification characteristics to add some depth to each entry. However, everything I have written is not to be taken too seriously. After all, this is gardening, not rocket science. So, no worries, no exams will follow. Have fun.

Aristolochia grandiflora

A-to-Z Vines

Tropaeolum peregrinum, habit. Photo by Suzy Bales.

Aconitum (a-con-eye′tum)
monkshood, wolfsbane
Ranunculaceae

Plants of this genus, with the rather gruesome common name of wolfsbane, are seldom thought of as climbers. The climbing wolfsbanes are not particularly popular for many reasons, one being that they don't actually climb, they scramble, much like a more civilized form of kudzu.

Aconitum volubile (vo-lew′bi-lee)
climbing monkshood
zones 2–6

This is the only species that is relatively easy to locate, but even it will require more than a little searching. Plants bear deeply lobed leaves on weak, scrambling stems up to 12 feet long. Where they grow well, such as in much of Canada, the northern states, and the West Coast, they produce 1 to 1½-inch-long flowers. The blue to purple flowers, occasionally tinged with green, occur from late summer into fall and are interesting and ornamental, if not spectacular. Plant them among vigorous shrubs like *Stephanandra* or spireas and allow them to climb through, over, and around the greenery. They are not suitable for trellises or other man-made devices.

As neat and entertaining as these plants are, they are anything but cooperative when they don't get their way. Make no mistake about it: this is a northern or West Coast plant. Cool nights and bright light are required to be at their best. If planted in too much shade, they look like bindweed, and in areas with too much heat, they will be dead in a year. Last, but certainly not least, all parts of the plant are poisonous, but the tuberous roots particularly so. It is hard to believe, but some people have mistaken them for garlic and ended up with more than smelly breath. Full sun, well-drained soils.

Propagation
Division in the spring or fall.

Method of climbing
None. Allow to scramble, or tie up as needed.

Etymology
Aconitum, from the Greek, *acŏnitŏn* (according to Pliny, a word applied to plants that grew "on steep rocks"); *volubile*, twining. Monkshood, derived from the shape of the flower; wolfsbane, the roots were used to poison wolves.

Actinidia (ak-tin-id′ ee-a)
Chinese gooseberry, kiwi
Actinidiaceae

Anyone who's ever enjoyed a kiwifruit has been the recipient of brilliant marketing. The large-leaved plants of *Actinidia deliciosa*, known as yang tao, were cultivated in China as long ago as the eighth century A.D. After visiting China in 1904, the headmistress of Wanganui Girls College brought seeds with her back to New Zealand, where they were grown by nurseryman Alexander Allison; by 1910, Chinese gooseberries, as they were known, were grown throughout the North Island. In 1952 the first shipment of fruit was sent to England; in 1959 they arrived in San Francisco, still under the name of Chinese gooseberry. The name did nothing to inspire sales, and after a few false starts, it was changed to kiwifruit, to enhance sales in United States and elsewhere. Sales took off slowly, and by 1970 aggressive promotion and marketing had made kiwis not only a household name but an "in" fruit. Today, kiwis are grown in many countries, not just New Zealand. Where frost is common, they are best grown in a greenhouse. If fruit is desired, plant one male for every seven females.

*Actinidia
kolomikta*

Most people are going to buy their kiwifruit at the market, but some might want to grow the variegated kiwi, *Actinidia kolomikta*, in the garden; it is a species sufficiently hardy for many temperate gardeners.

Actinidia kolomikta (kol-o-mik′ta)
variegated kiwi, cat vine
zones 4–8

These are woody vines and can become almost shrub like over time. They are far more cold hardy than many people give them credit for, overwintering in Minnesota and occasionally as far north as zone 3. It is one of the few plants I know that naturally bears variegated foliage, and (as the photo on page 15 shows), it is a wonderful plant to add color and texture to an old brick wall.

The ovate to oblong leaves are slightly fuzzy, and when grown in full sun, all or parts of the leaf will take on a brilliant white to pink coloration. The color is more dramatic in the spring and on plants grown in areas of cool (60–70F) nights in the summer. The peak impact for color is spring and perhaps again in the fall. If grown in shade or in warm climates, color will fade significantly.

The fragrant small white flowers are usually hidden by the large leaves, and the yellowish rounded hairy fruits may or may not be present. Plants of all kiwis are dioecious, meaning separate male and female plants occur. Most nursery-grown plants will be male, so little fruit should be expected.

Plants seem to affect cats the same way as catnip (*Nepeta*) does, so some protection from crazed felines may be necessary when plants are young.

Other species
Hardy kiwis (*Actinidia arguta*) are available, at least hardy to zone 7, perhaps colder, but these can be aggressive. My colleague Susan Harris, who gardens in Takoma Park, Maryland, writes on her excellent Sustainable Gardening Blog:

> Over the course of the summer I'll fill eight to ten full-size trash cans with the trimmings, and that's a lot of trimming. No wonder the standard advice is to prune it back *hard* in early spring—which I don't do because I'd have to retrain it to where I want it every year. After eight years it began producing flowers, but so far, no fruits have appeared.

Although the work is hard, she has to admit: "It's the most commented-on plant in my garden, hands down."

Actinidia pilosula has smaller and more narrow leaves than *A. kolomikta* but is easily identified by the white-tipped foliage and relatively large, pendulous

pink flowers. Plants of all kiwis can grow 20 feet tall. Zones 6–9.

Propagation
Take two- or three-node semi-hardwood cuttings in late summer. Provide bottom heat (70F).

Method of climbing
Support is necessary if training to climb up a trellis or wall.

Etymology
Actinidia, from the Greek, *aktis* ("ray"), referring to the pistils, which tend to radiate from the flowers; *deliciosa*, delicious; *kolomikta*, a local name from the Amur region of Asia; *pilosula*, somewhat hairy. Kiwi, cat plant, as above.

Actinidia arguta

Actinidia pilosula

Actinidia pilosula, flowers.
Photo by Jonathan Wright.

Adlumia (ad-loom'ee-a)

Fumariaceae

Two vines can be found in the genus, one native to Korea and one to eastern United States. Only the American species, *Adlumia fungosa*, is available, often only through seeds. Plants grow in a wide range, being native from northern Quebec to North Carolina and west to Manitoba. Unfortunately, plants are endangered, rare, or extinct in at least nine states.

Adlumia fungosa (fun-go'sa)

Allegheny fleece vine, climbing fumitory
zones 3–7

Plants in the fumitory family generally have flowers that look like bleeding hearts (*Dicentra*), so having a climber in the family is actually pretty neat. These are biennials, so the first-year plant will only be a short plant or a rosette of leaves, but in the spring of the second year, the long, climbing stems will occur.

Plants look a little like a climbing fern; the leaves are pinnately compound. The lower leaves may be as long as 10 inches, but uppermost leaves are

Adlumia
fungosa

significantly smaller. The stems, up to 10 feet in length, are best allowed to roam up, through, and over other plants, particularly those with dark green foliage, to allow the pale flowers to be shown off. Plants are not strong enough to stand on their own pergola or arbor.

The spongy pale pink, almost white flowers are borne in axillary clusters throughout the summer and fall. This will not be a plant that attracts you from a distance; the flowers are not flashy, and the leaves are rather light green. However, their subtlety is part of their beauty.

Plants are best for woodland areas, requiring consistent moisture and shady conditions. In fact, the foliage is a little wimpy and also requires protection from high winds.

Propagation
The only way to raise plants is from seeds, preferably collected from the plants and sown when ripe, or bought through a catalog. Place in containers that can go directly into the ground, as root damage can occur if roots are mishandled.

Method of climbing
Climbing is aided by the petioles, but initial help in getting stems to drape over other plants is necessary.

Etymology
Adlumia, for Major John Adlum (1759–1836), surveyor and associate judge, who had a 200-acre experimental farm in the Georgetown section of Washington, D.C., and was the first to sell Catawba grapes in America; *fungosa*, spongy, referring to the feel of the flowers. Allegheny fleece vine, from the area where it is found; climbing fumitory, fumitory refers to the botanical family.

Akebia (a-key′ bee-a)
chocolate vine
Lardizabalaceae

I have been teaching my students plant identification for many years and showing them the benefits of learning genus, specific epithet, common names, and family. When I look at this family name, perhaps I should take another look at my demands. Maybe a few of these little-seen, unpronounceable families are hardly worth the time for aspiring horticulturists. And then again, it does not hurt their education either. Two to five species may be found, native to Japan and China, with compound leaves of three or five leaflets.

Akebia quinata (quin-ah'ta)

fiveleaf akebia

zones 4–9

The slender stems bear alternate compound leaves of five stalked leaflets, each about 2 to 3 inches long. In good conditions, plants can grow 10 to 20 feet in height, essentially limited by the structure upon which they are trained. The individual small rose-red to purple-brown flowers are either male or female, and both are held in the same axillary raceme. The two or three female flowers are about 1 inch long with purple sepals and are found at the base of the inflorescence, while the eight to twelve smaller male flowers are paler purple, have reflexed sepals, and are at the tip. None of the flowers have petals, the color coming from the three sepals. Flowers open in the spring, and some people say they smell like chocolate; I find the fragrance more vanilla-like.

The fruit, which can be the most ornamental part of the plant, is a large, soft, sausage-shaped pod, 2 to 4 inches long, that develops in the fall. When ripe, it splits into three or four compartments, revealing cream-colored pulp that hides the many small black seeds. It may take quite a while for flowers to form, and vines may flower very inconsistently. If so, that may not be a bad thing. Unfortunately, as wonderful as this plant is, it has been reported to be invasive in Kentucky, Maryland, New Jersey, Pennsylvania, Virginia, and the

Akebia quinata, flowers.
Photo by Meg Green.

Akebia quinata, fruit.
Photo by Vincent Simeone.

District of Columbia. I suspect it has escaped in many other states as well. Plants are deciduous in colder climates but may be evergreen in zone 6 and above. If plants do not get out of hand, they are excellent for draping along fences and climbing arbors or into trees. If not given something upon which to climb, plants will be rampant groundcovers.

Plants tolerate full sun but appreciate some shade. Soil pH does not appear to be a problem.

'Alba' has white and purple flowers and is quite distinctive.

'Kohin-Nishiki' is quite rare. The plant has some variegated foliage and is a selection one either loves or dislikes. Variegated fans might want to give it a try.

Other species

Akebia trifoliata is similar in habit but not quite as vigorous and has only three leaflets. The male flowers are significantly smaller than the female flowers, and both are unscented. Hybrids between the two occur and have been designated as *A. ×pentaphylla*.

Propagation

From seed. If seed is stratified for about a month, germination will be improved. Softwood cuttings root well, but do better if provided with bottom heat (75F).

Method of climbing

Plants are twiners, using their long stems to loop around any structure or other stems.

Etymology

Akebia, Latinized version of the Japanese name, *akibi,* for these vines; *quinata,* in fives, referring to the leaflets; *trifoliata,* three leaflets. Chocolate vine, the flowers have a subtle scent of chocolate.

Allamanda (al-la-man'da)
Apocynaceae

These tropicals are referred to as vines but are really shrubs with long stems. Their popularity was long confined to conservatories and sunrooms in the North, but they are reasonably common sights as landscape plants in the southern United States. However, with the rage for more color and the trend toward smaller spaces, coupled with more widespread availability, they are becoming more popular outdoors throughout the entire country.

In their native habitat, they are often found in moist areas, such as the edge of rivers or swamps. Approximately twelve species occur, most being vine-like; but a number, like bush allamanda, *Allamanda schottii* (also known as *A. neriifolia*), are more shrub-like in habit. The fact is, where they are perennials, they all become quite woody over time. In temperate gardens, however, unless plants are overwintered under glass, only the basal stems are woody, while the flowering stems are vigorous and relatively soft. The most common species is *A. cathartica*, but cultivars of others are also offered. Purple allamanda, *A. blanchetii*, has 3- to 5-inch-long leaves in whorls of four, and rose-purple flowers. All are cold hardy into the low 30s to high 20s, although bush allamanda is likely a bit more cold tolerant, perhaps into the mid to mid to low 20s. They all need to be brought in below zone 9.

Many tropical plants like allamanda take some time to flower in the container or garden. This is not a problem but an opportunity for the landscaper and gardener to have something fresh in the garden during the lazy days of summer and into fall. As Dick Robrick of the exceptional Robrick Nursery in Hawthorne, Florida, states, "This delayed blooming is probably one of the reasons sales have not been too snappy on these plants. People buy them in spring and get tired of waiting for the flower. A little education might go a long way on these beautiful plants. If we use them as midsummer tropical specimens they can bring the Caribbean into the Chicago patio."

Allamanda cathartica (kath-ar'ti-ka)
golden trumpet
annual

This vigorous plant can grow 20 feet in a single season if summers are warm. The shiny green leaves are opposite to whorled, with wavy margins, and are wider at the top than at the base. The flowers are golden yellow, occasionally with white markings in the throat, and are produced in clusters (cymes) in summer and fall when night temperatures remain above 70F.

Full sun is needed, and lots of water, to get this vine established. Plants tolerate wet feet, but boggy soils are not necessary once growth begins. Pinch the new stems when plants are purchased to encourage basal growth. Aphids and whiteflies can be a problem, especially indoors.

'Brown Bud' has the same wonderful bright yellow blooms but flower buds that are tan to brown in color. Plants grow 8 to 10 feet tall.

'Hendersonii' has equally large yellow flowers and is one of the oldest selections in the trade.

Other cultivars

'Cherries Jubilee', a hybrid involving *Allamanda blanchetii*, grows 6 to 8 feet tall and bears rosy purple flowers, 3 to 4 inches wide, each with a black center.

'Compacta' bears handsome yellow flowers, shallow but wide, on plants less than 2 feet tall. It is likely a selection of or hybrid involving *Allamanda schottii*. The species itself is about 4 feet tall.

Allamanda cathartica 'Brown Bud'. Photo by Alan Shapiro.

Allamanda 'Cherries Jubilee'. Photo by Vincent Simeone.

Allamanda cathartica 'Hendersonii'

Propagation

Take two- or three-node softwood terminal cuttings, provide bottom heat (70F).

Method of climbing

None. Stems must be tied to supports or allowed to ramble over or through other plants.

Etymology

Allamanda, in honor of Swiss botanist Frédéric Allamand (1735–1795?), who sent seeds to Linnaeus; *cathartica*, purgative, cathartic, from the seeds. Golden trumpet, in reference to the flowers.

Ampelaster (am-pel-as′ter)
climbing aster
Asteraceae

Whoever thinks of asters as vines? To most gardeners, asters are fall-flowering bushes that often get weedy and untidy, but certainly not vines. The climbing aster, *Ampelaster carolinianus* (long known as *Aster carolinianus*), is actually a scraggly shrub but is treated as a climber simply because of the long stems produced. The plant is softly hairy throughout and in the fall produces pink daisy flowers with narrow ray segments and yellow centers. Flowers occur mainly at the end of the stems. One of the plant's biggest drawbacks is its late flowering; it may not start to flower until mid October, a little too late for areas with early frosts. Cold hardiness is likely zone 7.

I have grown this plant in my north Georgia garden, and it is more fun to tell people about than it is eye-catching. The plant produces far more stems and leaves than flowers, and the long wait can be disappointing. However, this may reflect on my horticulture skills, as I have also seen a wonderful specimen in the garden of Ann Armstrong, a talented gardener, obviously a better one than I, in Charlotte, North Carolina.

Propagation

The easiest method is one- or two-node terminal cuttings taken in early summer. They root readily in warm, moist conditions.

Method of climbing

Plants produce 4- to 8-foot-tall stems, much like "climbing" roses, that must be tied or trained. There are no self-supporting tissues.

Ampelaster carolinianus, habit

Ampelaster carolinianus

Etymology

Ampelaster, from the Greek, *ampelos* ("grape vine") and *aster* ("star"), resembling but inferior to aster; *carolinianus*, from North or South Carolina. Climbing aster, self-explanatory.

Ampelopsis (am-pel-op'sis)
porcelain vine
Vitaceae

About twenty-five species of these shrubs or vines occur, generally with tendrils opposite the leaves. The foliage may be simple or compound, and plants are far better known for their beautiful fruit rather than their small greenish flowers. Although a number are ornamental vines, only one, *Ampelopsis brevipedunculata*, is grown in North America.

Ampelopsis brevipedunculata (brev-ee-peh-dunk-ew-lah'ta)
porcelain vine
zones 4–8

I have come across this vine on numerous travels, particularly in northern gardens or in Europe. Walking under these rampant leafy growers in the summer is a thrill, as the green stems, bearing alternate, somewhat heart-shaped, hairy leaves, climb like a grape vine. In the fall, however, the mature small bright blue to cyan fruits are held like grape clusters and are easily the most visible part of the plant. Plants may be cut to the ground each year as flowers occur on new growth.

Unfortunately, plants have a well-deserved reputation of being invasive as those wonderful little berries are dispersed and new vines appear throughout the garden like magic. Comments like these—"It blocks the sun," from a New York gardener; "It is impossible to eradicate," from a frustrated fellow in Maryland; the simple heartfelt plea of a Floridian, "It is a nightmare here, help!!"—pretty much summarize the problem. In case you think I am making this stuff up, turns out the City of Chicago also recently banned this plant from being imported or sold. The spreading tendency is not a problem in some areas, but I recommend talking to other gardeners or extension people in your area before planting. We don't need another kudzu.

As much as I do enjoy a well-grown porcelain vine, it has other problems that may keep it out of the garden anyway. It seems to be filet mignon for Japanese beetles, which can chew it full of holes in no time flat. A number of leaf fungal diseases are also known to bother the foliage. As you can see, this is not one of my favorite plants.

'Elegans' is quite popular due to the green and white variegated leaves, tinged pink upon emergence, and its red petioles, one of its most ornamental characteristics. It is less rampant, so some say it may be less invasive. I rather doubt it.

var. *maximowiczii* has handsome deeply lobed leaves. As vigorous and as invasive as the species.

Other species

Ampelopsis arborea, pepper vine, is most common in the South, producing pinnately compound 4- to 7-inch-long leaves, shiny on the upperside, somewhat hairy when young beneath. The dark purple fruit is almost as lovely as that of porcelain vine, but plants can be aggressive pests. Great for smothering abandoned houses but may not be good for neighborly relationships. Zones 7–9.

Ampelopsis brevipedunculata

*Ampelopsis
brevipedunculata
'Elegans'*

Propagation

Seed may be germinated readily if sown in soil, then stratified for a month at 40F for about a month. Semi-hardwood cuttings root easily if provided with bottom heat. If more plants are needed, visit a gardener who put one in the ground about three years ago.

Method of climbing

Plants have tendrils, just like grapes.

Etymology

Ampelopsis, from the Greek, *ampelos* ("grape vine") and *psis* ("looks like"), from its resemblance to the grape vine; *arborea*, treelike, woody; *brevipedunculata*, short flower stalk. Porcelain vine, in reference to the color of the fruit; pepper vine, the fruits are edible and have a somewhat peppery taste.

Antigonon (an-tig'oh-non)
   Polygonaceae

There are only about three species in this tropical genus, and only one is available at all. However, the coral vine, *Antigonon leptopus*, is well worth searching out. It is as vigorous as plants of knotweed, *Polygonum*, but better behaved and far more ornamental.

Antigonon leptopus (lep-top′us)

coral vine
annual

Coral vine gets my vote as one of the prettier vines in the garden. By no means does it knock your socks off, but its vigor and coral-pink flowers in late summer are a delight. In the tropics, the vigor of the plant has taken on mythical properties; plants grew so quickly they were used as camouflage to hide anti-aircraft guns in the Second World War. If it can hide such monstrosities, think what it would do for the garbage shed or broken-down wreck in the front yard. Most of us don't live in the tropics, so perhaps the old Volkswagen may not be completely hidden, but plants still climb readily on an arbor, even as far north as Racine.

The coral-pink to rose flowers are held in long racemes and, once started, continue for months. The thin stems are obviously zig-zaggy, like many members of the family. Flowers form as vines mature, so flowering may not occur

Antigonon leptopus, habit. Photo by Meg Green.

Antigonon leptopus.
Photo by Alan
Shapiro.

Antigonon leptopus
'Alba'. Photo by Alan
Shapiro.

in the North until late summer or fall, in the South (below zone 7), flowers occur in summer.

'Alba' bears clean white flowers and grows almost as vigorously. It is difficult to find but well worth the effort.

Propagation
Take two- or three-node softwood terminal cuttings, provide bottom heat (70F).

Method of climbing
Stems twist and tendrils occur in the axils of the stems, but some support is useful if training to climb up a trellis. They are often used to advantage growing over other shrubs.

Etymology
Antigonon, from the Greek, *anti* ("in place of") and *polygŏnŏn* ("knot-weed"), indicating its similarity to *Polygonum*; *leptopus*, fine-stalked. Coral vine, in reference to the color of the flowers.

Aristolochia (a-ris-tow-low' kee-a)
birthwort, pipe vine
Aristolochiaceae

I have written about the pipe vines for other publications, and each time I come to the subject, I find I have more to share. For example, how can you not like a genus that includes such a range, from plants that crawl slowly along the ground (*Aristolochia clematitis*) to vigorous screeners (*A. macrophylla*) and those with wonderful stinky monstrous flowers (*A. grandiflora*). The bizarre flowers are unique in not having recognizable petals or sepals. They act as insect traps as well because of the short downward-pointing hairs leading to the pistil which allow insects in but not out. Soon the stamens shed their pollen on the flies, and the hairs wither, allowing the insects to seek another pipe and do it all over again. It must be exhausting for the flies, to be sure.

Flowers of most species are malodorous, some violently so, and without doubt, all are interesting. The genus consists of about 300 species, so if you want to be a collector, knock yourself out. They are much more fun to collect than salvias, that's for sure. At least half a dozen are native to the United States, but regardless of provenance, most gardeners likely know only a couple.

The most available by far is *Aristolochia macrophylla*, simply because it is the most cold hardy. We have tried a few other species in the Trial Gardens at UGA; occasionally one or two come back, but we treat them as annuals nevertheless.

Plants have large fleshy underground roots or rhizomes and are best moved when dormant.

Aristolochia littoralis (lit-or-al' lis)
calico flower
zones 8–11

This vigorous climber is almost as aggressive as our native Dutchman's pipe but differs in having smaller leaves and far larger flowers—so large that people will stop and exclaim about this really weird-looking flower. The 3-inch-wide flowers are borne on long, thin flower stalks and open purple blotched with white, usually yellow in the center. Even the whitish buds are quite spectacular, particularly as they expand prior to opening.

Many people suggest that this species bears some of the least malodorous flowers, but odor is in the nostrils of the sniffer. Having stuck my nose in

Aristolochia littoralis. Photo by Alan Shapiro.

many of them, I smell little, but when I crushed the leaves, they were rather unpleasant.

Plants self-sow readily in tropical areas, particularly where moist soils occur; however, this is seldom a problem in temperate climates. The Florida Nurserymen and Greenhouse Association (FNGA) and the Tampa Bay Wholesale Growers (TBWG), in cooperation with the Florida Exotic Pest Plant Council (FLEPPC), have asked Florida nursery growers, landscape professionals, and garden center retailers to voluntarily stop propagating and selling *Aristolochia littoralis*.

Aristolochia macrophylla (mak-ro′fill-a)
Dutchman's pipe
zones 4–8

Long known and still sold as *Aristolochia durior*, this reliable climber is appreciated more for its foliage than its flowers. The kidney- to heart-shaped leaves, 10 to 12 inches wide, make a wonderful screen or climber for the porch or garden wall. Twenty to thirty feet of growth in one season is not uncommon. There are other species with far more interesting flowers, but this is my choice for bodacious, handsome foliage.

The yellow-greenish flowers are far smaller (1 to 2 inches long) than the mammoth leaves. Each flares to form three brownish purple lobes and has the distinctive pipe-like shape, but they are often obscured by the foliage, and flowers are only slightly fragrant. Plants are native to the Appalachians in the southeastern United States but can handle garden climates as far north as

Aristolochia
macrophylla

Aristolochia
macrophylla, flower.
Photo by Suzy Bales.

upstate New York and into protected areas of southern and eastern Canada, even into zone 3.

Lastly, this species is the main plant food for pipe vine swallowtail butterflies, so expect the leaves to be chewed on occasionally. The holes are for a good cause.

Other species

There are a number of South American species with large interesting flowers, and from a distance they are not easy to distinguish.

Aristolochia grandiflora bears flowers that have been measured up to 30 inches from top to bottom; usually they are brown in the center, smell quite awful, and have a long, thin tail trailing from the base of the flower. *Aristolochia gigantea* has similar flowers, but not as large as those of *A. grandiflora* and with a shorter tail. The smell is not unpleasant, at least to my nose. Both should be treated as annuals.

Aristolochia sempervirens is a wonderful evergreen plant that can be trained as a climber. Small lustrous heart-shaped leaves are carried on long petioles, and the small flowers are yellow with purple stripes and borne on racemes, perhaps a dozen at a time. Plants are native to the Mediterranean area in Europe and should be considered annual in most parts of North America.

Aristolochia tomentosa grows 20 feet tall and is a fuzzy version of *A. macrophylla* with somewhat smaller leaves. Also an excellent food source for the pipe vine swallowtail butterfly. Zones 4–9.

Aristolochia trilobata, birthwort, has wonderfully three-lobed glossy leaves

Aristolochia grandiflora, flower buds

Aristolochia sempervirens

and small flowers that look like a cross between a jack-in-the-pulpit and a pipevine. Each flower has the same pipe-like look seen in others but includes a long purple "tail." An annual (zone 9) in most of the country, but worth a try for something in the weird category.

Propagation
Take two- or three-node softwood terminal cuttings, use a rooting hormone, and provide bottom heat (70F). Root cuttings have also been successful. If propagating from seed, soak seeds for forty-eight hours, then cold stratify (35F) for approximately three months.

Method of climbing
Stems twist and tendrils occur in the axils of the stems, but some support is useful if training to climb up a trellis.

Etymology
Aristolochia, from the Greek, *aristos* ("best") and *lochos*, concerning birth, in reference to the purported value of some species in childbirth; *grandiflora*, large-flowered; *gigantea*, large, giant; *littoralis*, of the seashore; *macrophylla*, large leaf; *sempervirens*, evergreen; *tomentosa*, densely hairy, often with matted hairs; *trilobata*, three-lobed. Birthwort, flowers of some species (*A. clematitis*) were thought to resemble fetuses and were used as a calmative during childbirth; calico flower comes from the purplish brown pattern reminiscent of calico fabric; Dutchman's pipe, in reference to the slender S-shaped curving tube of the flower.

Asarina (a-sah-reen'a)
climbing snapdragon
Scrophulariaceae

I have been growing climbing snapdragons for many years, with mixed success. There are about sixteen species, mostly native to Mexico and southwestern United States. The flowers are similar to the open-mouthed tubular flowers of snapdragons, with five broad petals, but differ dramatically in habit. In my opinion, the easiest and most prolific species is trailing snapdragon, *Asarina procumbens*, but it is better known as a plant for rock gardens or as a trailer; it is not a natural vine.

The vining species such as *Asarina antirrhiniflora*, *A. barclaiana*, and others can be quite vigorous but also are susceptible to diseases if conditions are challenging. Plants are annuals in most of the country.

Some taxonomists have moved *Asarina* to *Maurandya*; however, since there is still considerable disagreement as to the validity of the change, I will leave the genus here for now.

Asarina antirrhiniflora (an-tir-rine-i-floor'a)

climbing snapdragon, roving sailor
zones 9–11

I love snapdragons, so I was immediately intrigued with a snapdragon that could climb. I procured some seed, watched them germinate, then planted them alongside a fence. And waited, and waited. They were slow to climb, that is for sure; perhaps they were planted too early, or perhaps the soils were not to their liking. The leaves are held on very thin stems, and are ovate to hastate, alternate, heart-shaped at the base, and pointed at the end (acuminate). The tubular flowers are about 1 inch wide, two-lipped, like a snapdragon, and generally pale to dark purple. Look inside the flower; you will see a small structure, referred to as a palate, which appears to close the mouth. You will also notice that the entire inside of the flower is white tinged with yellow. Plants bloom in mid to late summer and continue on and off through fall.

Plants are native to hot, arid areas in Texas and Mexico and occasionally will be seen in areas with limestone soils, suggesting a higher pH may be useful. In areas of California, they seem to produce many flowers for a long period of time; however, further east, they are often slow to grow and disappointing in flower, perhaps because of humidity or too much heat. This species may be better as a conservatory specimen.

It is hard to know what cultivars actually belong to what species, but cultivars indeed are sold.

'Bride's White' bears white flowers. This may be the same as 'Bridal Bouquet'.

'Joan Loraine' is a popular cultivar, bearing purple flowers with a white throat.

'Magic Dragon' produces handsome scarlet flowers.

'Mystic Pink' has deeper pink to rose flowers.

'Pink Ice' has flowers of light pink.

Other species

It is quite difficult to see the difference between species.

Asarina barclaiana (Mexican viper) and *A. scandens* (twining snapdragon) are available through seed catalogs and occasionally as plants online. The former differs from *A. antirrhiniflora* by having a more obvious triangular leaf and larger flowers with hairy sepals. The petals are usually white to pink then

Asarina 'Joan Loraine'

Asarina 'Mystic Pink'

darken to a deep purple. *Asarina scandens* is similar to *A. barclaiana* except that the sepals are smooth and flowers are usually lavender.

Asarina lophospermum, otherwise known as lophos, appeared with much fanfare, in its selection 'Wine Red', a few years ago under the name of *Lophospermum scandens*. Taxonomists are still divided, and it usually appears under the latter name. The flowers of 'Wine Red' are large and exquisitely wine-red; the dark green foliage, heart-shaped and serrated. In the greenhouse or protected areas it is quite spectacular, sufficiently vigorous to grow alongside sweet potato vine and other rampant plants. However, outdoor performance did not live up to the billing. If you can find it, it is still worth a try, especially in the West Coast states.

Propagation
Take one- or two-node softwood terminal cuttings from nonflowering shoots in late summer, use a rooting hormone, and provide bottom heat (70F). Root cuttings have also been successful. Seed propagation is reasonably easy. Germinate inside in spring, and put plants out in late spring to early summer.

Method of climbing
Stems twist and plants climb around thin structures or through chicken wire on fences.

Etymology
Asarina, Spanish vernacular name for *Antirrhinum*; *Maurandya*, named for Spanish botanist Catalina Patcratia Maurandy, wife of the director of the Car-

Asarina barclaiana.
Photo by Meg Green.

Asarina lophospermum

tagena Botanic Garden; *antirrhiniflora*, flowers resembling snapdragon; *scandens*, climbing. Climbing snapdragon, self-explanatory.

Basella (ba-sel′la)
Basellaceae

I have grown one representative of this genus, Malabar spinach, for many years at the Trial Gardens at UGA, and it has always fascinated me. Spinach on a vine, who would have thought? *Basella alba* has green stems; var. *rubra*, a more handsome form, produces shiny, dark green spinach-like leaves all along its twining red stems. However, many authorities claim that Malabar spinach should correctly be called *B. rubra*. Nearly all vines I have seen have obvious red stems. The small pink flowers, bunched together like tiny bananas, are cute but almost hidden in the foliage. The flowers, however, are soon transformed into shiny black fruit. It is, all in all, a neat and novel vine and a great conversation piece.

I was fascinated by the common name, partly because I wondered if the plant really was a substitute for spinach, while trying to recall my geography as to where Malabar was. First of all, it turns out that this spinach is indeed consumed; in fact, both the leaves and stems are eaten. The most common method of cooking is as a pot herb, mixed in a stew with meat or other vegetables. The leaves have a mild flavor, or are almost tasteless. The stems may be somewhat bitter and become gelatinous or mucilaginous, especially when

Basella alba var. *rubra*, flowers

Basella alba var. *rubra*, fruit

Basella alba
var. *rubra*

overcooked. The leaves are a good source of vitamins A and C, calcium, and iron. It turns out that Malabar spinach is one of the rapidly growing leaf vegetables in some tropical regions. As for Malabar, it is a region of southwestern India, lying between the Western Ghats, a range of hills parallel to the Arabian Sea, and the Arabian Sea itself.

Plants are easy to grow. Providing structures on which the stems can twist and twine will allow the plants to attain heights of 15 feet or more in a single season. The plants won't knock you out with flower or fruit power, but the lustrous shiny leaves are really quite handsome. One drawback is the tendency to reseed. I do not consider the plant as much a nuisance as morning glory; however, it can reappear where you least expect it.

Propagation
The quickest and easiest method is by seed. Soak seeds overnight before sowing.

Method of climbing
Stems twist and plants climb around thin structures or through chicken wire on fences.

Etymology
Basella, Latinized version of the vernacular name; *alba*, white, in reference to the whitish stems. Malabar spinach, as explained earlier, also native to Ceylon, or presently Sri Lanka.

Berberidopsis (ber-ber-i-dop'sis)
coral plant
Flacourtiaceae

I admit to including many vines that are personal favorites but are little known, difficult to find, and for some areas, even more difficult to grow. That I write about such plants explains why my books seldom make the bestseller lists.

I first saw *Berberidopsis corallina* in the garden of Helen Dillon in Dublin, Ireland. I did not know the plant, but I was certainly not alone. However, since Helen receives about 150 visitors a day, it soon became known to many gardeners around the world. Plants make vigorous evergreen climbers; the foliage ranges from dull to glossy dark green above and bluish green below. However, it is the brilliant scarlet-red flowers that catch the eye. One writer described the color as "crimson to deep sealing-wax red." The rounded fleshy blossoms are held on long, pendulous racemes, each flower stem about 1 inch long, and persist for many weeks.

Berberidopsis corallina, flowers

Berberidopsis corallina

Plants are native to Chile, and unfortunately, there don't appear to be many sources for this plant. Occasionally seeds are offered, but that is normal for many of these little-known vines. They are cold hardy likely to about zone 7, but heat tolerance is also an issue. However, let's find some plants or seeds and give them a try. I am on the hunt, as I write.

Propagation

Take semi-softwood cuttings; use mist and bottom heat (70–72F). Seeds may also be tried, but germination is erratic. Some gardeners have been successful with soil layering, that is, burying a portion of the stem in soil and allowing the plant to root at the nodes.

Method of climbing

It is a scrambler, occasionally twisting around structures, but it is at its best growing through conifers or large shrubs.

Etymology

Berberidopsis, from *Berberis* (barberry) and the Greek, *ŏpsis* ("looks like")—the foliage perhaps (but not much else) bears some resemblance to barberry; *corallina*, coral-red, referring to the color of the flowers. Coral plant, again, in reference to the flower color.

Bignonia (big-known′ee-a)

cross vine
Bignoniaceae

Bignoniaceae includes over 100 genera of large-flowered plants such as *Campsis*, *Catalpa*, *Jacaranda*, and *Tecoma*. The genus has ebbed and flowed, at one time containing more than 150 species, or two, with various numbers in between. The debate has been going on for decades, but most taxonomists now agree that the genus consists of a single species, *Bignonia capreolata*, native to the southeastern United States. Plants have beautiful flowers, opposite evergreen compound leaves, and long stems, which, in cross-section, show a four-parted or cross-like arrangement.

Generally when I have looked at the flowers of naturally occurring cross vines for more than thirty seconds, I have a sore neck and strained eyes from staring at flowers high in trees or even perched atop chimneys (see opposite). These vines will climb over 50 feet and then flower only at the top. Sometimes the only way I knew there was a cross vine growing was from the flowers that were shed on the ground in the spring. However, with a little help, they can be trained on a fence, or even on mailboxes (pity the poor carrier), and the flowers and foliage can be enjoyed.

*Bignonia
capreolata*

The leaves often consist of only one pair of stalked leaflets, each pointed at the tip and heart-shaped at the base. Between the two leaflets are coiled tendrils ending in small discs that allow plants to climb on trees, concrete, or brick. The five-lobed flowers are flared at the end and usually held in few-flowered inflorescences. The trumpet-shaped flowers peak in the spring and range from deep orange to almost scarlet, but I usually find them a dirty brownish orange-red. However, some of the offered cultivars are really quite eye-catching.

Gardeners have found that restricting the roots by planting in large containers, for example, reduces the vigor of the plant and encourages flowering at heights that may be enjoyed. Alternatively, cutting back the previous year's growth by two-thirds is also recommended, if you remember. Or, simply, just build a short structure.

Plants are relatively disease-free but can be quite susceptible to mealybugs. Plants can also sucker at a considerable distance from the mother plant. Mow them down.

Bignonia capreolata, flowers.
Photo by Meg Green.

var. *atrosanguinea* has deeper redder flowers than *Bignonia capreolata*.

'Dragon Lady' has rich, ruby-red flowers. The dark green leaves turn a handsome purple in the winter. A winner of the prestigious Pennsylvania Horticultural Society's Gold Medal Plant Award in 2003.

'Jekyll' provides vigorous growth with handsome salmon-orange flowers.

'Tangerine Beauty' is a lovely color, with tangerine petal tube and a yellow center.

Propagation

Usually by seed. Collect the seeds from late summer through fall when they are light brown and beginning to dry. Seeds remain viable one year in sealed, refrigerated containers.

Method of climbing

Plants climb by clinging tendrils.

Etymology

Bignonia, in honor of Abbé Jean-Paul Bignon (1662–1743), librarian to Louis XIV; *capreolata*, provided with tendrils. Cross vine, in reference to the cross-like arrangement of stems in cross section.

Bignonia capreolata 'Jekyll'. Photo by Robert Bowden.

Bignonia capreolata 'Tangerine Beauty'. Photo by Alan Shapiro.

Bougainvillea (boo-gan-vil′lee-a)

Nyctaginaceae

These large shrubs (*Bougainvillea spectabilis*, *B. glabra*) that masquerade as vines in the tropics are not often grown as garden plants in North America, other than in favored locales like southern California and Florida. That bougainvillea is a tropical vine is not a problem; however, the fact that it must be mature to flower, relegates it to the conservatory for most gardeners. The cascading blooms in the conservatory at Longwood Gardens are a perfect example. This is not the easiest plant to site, particularly if you live in un-Hawaii like places such as Ohio or Michigan. In their native habitat, day and night length are approximately the same, and flowering will take place year-round. For most gardeners, it is best purchased and treated like a high-priced annual.

If purchasing from the garden store, select actively growing plants in a relatively large container. Place the plants in the sunniest location in the garden. If you want to bring the plant indoors in the fall, place it in a container you can transport without hurting your back, or bury the pot so it can be removed in the fall. If coming from a conservatory, don't be too impatient to put plants

Bougainvillea at Longwood Gardens

out, as damage may occur if night temperatures dip. Allow the plants to acclimate for a week before putting them in the final summer location. Transplant to a place that is too hot and too bright for any sane person, and allow those golden rays to saturate the plant. Plants are full-sun lovers; a western exposure to bake the plants may be perfect.

Once they start to vigorously grow, they should be cut back to encourage new growth. Try to keep all shoots about 20 inches long. They flower on new wood, and once pinched, they take about fifty days to flower on that new growth. This is a bit of a problem in places like Montreal or Minot, where fifty days above 80F is a rare treat. Use a trellis support in the container or garden, but if plants are pinched to avoid long, vegetative shoots, an elaborate support will not be needed. Tie the new shoots to the trellis.

In the fall, if you decide to bring it in the house, expect massive leaf drop as plants try to acclimate to the new and less favorable environment. They will put on new leaves but will flower poorly, if at all, while inside. Some people simply store them in a heated (45–50F) garage or something similar to keep them alive until the next spring. Plants may be pruned before bringing in, but I recommend waiting for temperatures to warm up in early spring and doing it then.

The leaves of bougainvillea are smooth and carried on shoots that can be quite spiny. The bloom color is based on the color of the papery bracts that surround the small white flower.

There are dozens of cultivars, in flower colors from purples to white and even some with variegated leaves; however, what is available in the store may be disappointing. Two good sites for bougainvillea cultivars are Southeast Texas Gardening (www.southeasttexasgardening.info/growboug.htm) and Gordon Braswell's Web page (www.southeasttexasgardening.info/bouginfo.htm).

Propagation
By node cuttings only. Take two- or three-node cuttings in warm seasons and root under mist and warm (70–75F) root temperatures.

Method of climbing
It is a shrub with long, rambling shoots. If grown outdoors it may be tied to a trellis; however, if not pruned in a temperate climate, it will not flower well before frost.

Etymology
Bougainvillea, named in honor of Louis Antoine de Bougainville (1729–1811), noted mathematician, scientist, musician, and soldier, as well as Fellow of

Bougainvillea
with purple
bracts. Photo by
Alan Shapiro.

Bougainvillea with
pink-tinged white
bracts. Photo by Alan
Shapiro.

Bougainvillea
'Raspberry Ice'

the Royal Society of London, who sailed around the world in 1767–69; *glabra*, without hairs; *spectabilis*, spectacular, showy.

Campsis (kamp′sis)
  trumpet vine
  Bignoniaceae

I remember seeing my first campsis growing up a wall, covered in orange trumpet flowers and at least 30 feet tall, on the campus of Michigan State University in East Lansing. The following week I was given an assignment to write about a native plant and to submit leaves, flowers, and stems of that plant. The explicit directions stated, "Take no material from the campus." I guess I must not have seen those words. My excellent treatise on *Campsis radicans* was trashed by the professor because I'd innocently collected material from that wonderful vine. I even labeled the location. Oh well, such are the ways plants get into our heads.

A number of species occur, the most common being *Campsis radicans*, native to eastern United States, followed by *C. grandiflora*, from Asia, along with a number of cultivars and hybrids. They are all vigorous, extraordinary in flower and eye-popping when mature. If that is not enough, they are like magnets to hummingbirds.

Full sun is needed, and in many cases patience is a bonus. It may take three years before flowers occur, and if soils are rich, plants may become big and rambunctious, but with nary a flower. Also, root suckers can spread the plants without invitation. These are plants for the tough gardener; be a wuss, and they will run roughshod over you.

Campsis radicans (rad′i-cans)
  trumpet creeper
  zones 5–9

How this plant can grow! They are shrubs with long, flowing branches that must be supported to buildings or posts, but once established they will eat stucco walls and telephone poles for breakfast. This is not for the meek or fainthearted.

The species produces opposite compound leaves with nine to eleven serrated leaflets, each leaflet 2 to 3 inches long. The narrow campanulate flowers are light orange with a yellow throat and up to 3 inches long. They occur four to twelve to a cluster, each flower with rounded lobes at the top and a short calyx. The long fruit can be up to 4 inches long and releases many two-winged seeds. For the first year or two of cultivation, cut plants back hard to establish more basal shoots and better basal branching. As plants mature, they will send out aerial roots to make you think twice about cutting it down.

This is a beautiful plant and where properly grown is incredible. However, it can be a problem restraining this plant; here are a couple of postings, the first from New York, the second from Michigan, from Dave's Garden (davesgarden.com), an excellent Web site.

> To add to the insult it only gave me one flower for all of the trouble it has caused! We tried digging it up but after a three-foot trench around the house and with endless [. . .] tubers and roots of it that we yanked out with *much* work, we gave up. There is still more of this creature spreading its tentacles around my gardens.

> As beautiful as the flowers are it is the most invasive plant I have ever dealt with. It has taken over my back yard, and [I] am now finding shoots 300 feet away.

Campsis radicans. Photo by Vincent Simeone.

The moral of these tales? Think twice before purchasing, and be ruthless in pruning.

'Crimson Trumpet' bears deep velvety red flowers. Equally vigorous.

'Judy' has large yellow flowers.

'Praecox' produces scarlet-red flowers.

'Yellow Trumpet' (var. *flava*) has pale green leaves and deep yellow flowers.

Other species and cultivars

Campsis grandiflora does not grow as vigorously, only to about 15 feet, which may be the best thing about it. It produces a loose inflorescence of orange flowers with yellow inside and more deeply cut lobes at the top of the flower. It also differs by having only four to seven leaflets and few aerial roots. A number of wonderful cultivars have been established including 'Morning Calm', which grows 8 to 12 feet and produces orange-red flowers in abundant clusters during the summer and fall. Plants caught the attention of the Pennsylvania Horticultural Society, who awarded it a 2002 Gold Medal Plant for its outstanding qualities and performance in the mid-Atlantic states. It is hardier than most *C. grandiflora* types, down to zone 6. 'Thunbergii' has orange flowers with reflexed lobes. Plants are hardy only to zone 7.

Campsis ×*tagliabuana*, a hybrid of *C. grandiflora* and *C. radicans*, is intermediate between the two species. The flowers are orange on the outside and scarlet inside. 'Coccinea' has scarlet flowers. 'Indian Summer' is superb, showing off glowing apricot-orange flowers on a large vigorous plant. 'Jersey Peach' has beautiful peach-colored flowers. 'Minnesota Red' bears deep red flowers, parentage unknown. 'Madame Galen' enjoys great popularity because of her somewhat restrained habit and her deep apricot flowers and dark green foliage. Plants enjoy many positive comments, but they too have their fair share of critics.

Propagation

Plants can be propagated by digging root suckers if they occur. Cuttings from flowering shoots may be rooted; they produce flowers faster than cuttings on immature shoots. Seed germinates well if given a six-week cold treatment at 40F prior to sowing in warm, moist conditions.

Method of climbing

It is a vigorous shrub with long, rambling shoots and no self-climbing structures, and must be trained to a strong structure. As plants mature, shoots will grow through existing stems to stay upright. If not supported, a groundcover will result.

Etymology

Campsis, from the Greek, *kampe* ("something bent"), referring to the curved stamens in the flowers; *grandiflora*, large flowers; *radicans*, having rooting stems, in reference to the aerial roots; *tagliabuana*, honors the Tagliabue brothers, Alberto and Carlo, nurserymen from Lainate, near Milan, 1858. Trumpet, in reference to the shape of the flowers.

Campsis ×*tagliabuana*
'Indian Summer'

Campsis ×*tagliabuana*
'Indian Summer', habit

Canavalia (kan-a-val′ee-a)

sword bean

Fabaceae

Although there are over fifty species in this genus, few are easy to find. They are cultivated in tropical and subtropical regions for soil improvement (they add nitrogen) and for forage for livestock. They are not grown abundantly as the beans contain a mild toxin. If consumed by humans, the fruit must be boiled to get rid of the toxins. Young foliage is also edible.

Canavalia gladiata (glad-ee-ah′ta)

Jack bean

annual

I must say I really have come to enjoy this annual bean, because it is so easy to grow, it is a great screening plant, and because I can tell such wonderful stories about it. Plants grow wonderfully fast, 10 to 12 feet high in a season, but are not invasive, nor will they pull down structures like wisteria or campsis do. It is my choice for Jack's bean in the "Jack and the Beanstalk" fable. I can see Jack's mother tossing the large seeds out her cottage window; these plants

Canavalia gladiata, flower

Canavalia gladiata, seed pods. Photo by Meg Green.

germinate and grow so quickly, they could be growing through the clouds the very next day. It is wonderful to see eyes of children open wide as they stand beside the plant, and watch their imaginations come alive. We don't grow many of these vines in the Trial Gardens at UGA, but we try to keep at least one in the garden to remind us of being a child.

The seeds should be planted when temperatures are warm. Planting too early in the spring is simply a waste of time. The trifoliate leaves (in threes) consist of leaflets, each about 5 inches in length and pointed like a sword. Plants grow quickly and climb on their own if provided with something like chicken wire or lattice. They are useful as a screen but if nothing else, they can be enjoyed simply as an ornamental vine. The pink flowers are small (1 to 1½ inches long) relative to the size of the plant but are quite handsome; however, these small flowers give rise to enormous fruit, about 2½ inches across and easily 15 inches long. They are deep green, but when they mature, they are filled with half a dozen or more brilliantly coral-colored seeds. We gather the seeds in the fall and keep them for next year's crop.

Other species
Canavalia ensiformis, wonder bean, is similar but has somewhat more narrow leaves and more narrow (1-inch-wide), smaller beans. The seeds are white. This could also be Jack's bean; there are no data, so have fun with the children.

Propagation
Collect seeds from the beans in the fall. They may be stored in plastic bags in a relatively dry area. Plant the following spring in prepared soil, outside, after all threat of frost has passed. Some claim that soaking for twelve hours before planting enhances germination, but we have not noticed a difference.

Method of climbing
Plants produce wiry stems that intertwine through other stems and in and around fencing or lattice work. A little help tying stems when plantlets are young accelerates the vining habit.

Etymology
Canavalia, Latinized version of the Malabar (see *Basella*) vernacular name *kanavali*; *ensiformis*, quite straight and with a sharp point like a sword; *gladiata*, swordlike. Jack bean, not sure where this came from, may be in reference to Jack, but doubtful; wonder bean, referring to its rapid growth rate; sword bean, in reference to the shape of the leaflets.

Cardiospermum (kard-ee-o-spur′mum)
heartseed
Sapindaceae

Storytelling is an art and a bit of a skill. I just mentioned that the beans of *Canavalia* are terrific for storytelling, particularly for children, but the plants in this genus are designed to make all people smile. The most common species is *Cardiospermum halicacabum*, balloon vine, also known as love-in-a-puff. The plant itself, while interesting to look at, is just as easily ignored when walking by it. I do enjoy the vine; it grows rapidly, climbs by itself, and produces ferny light green foliage on branched stems. The white flowers are small and not particularly ornamental, but they give rise to some wonderful inflated fruit.

The rounded, puffy fruits are three-sided and almost a translucent green, also easily overlooked, cute but forgettable . . . until you show people the seeds within. Inside are the three black seeds, each with an obvious, white heart-shaped spot. As I reveal the "love-in-a puff," people literally say, "Wow" (or other such clever comment). Never have I demonstrated these without a garden full of smiles.

Cardiospermum
halicacabum

Plants will reseed and can be a bit of a nuisance; they are easily pulled up if you don't want them, so I don't consider them invasive.

Other species

Cardiospermum grandiflorum, heartseed, differs by giving larger flowers (1 inch wide) and ellipsoidal fruit. Love-in-an-ellipsoid doesn't run off the tongue as well.

Propagation

Collect seeds from the puffs whenever they are ripe. The seeds are ripe when they turn black. They may be stored in plastic bags in a relatively dry area. Plant in prepared soil outside after all threat of frost has passed next spring.

Method of climbing

Plants produce tendrils that catch on wire or thin lattice.

Etymology

Cardiospermum, from the Greek, *kardia* ("heart") and *sperma* ("seed"), in reference to the story above; *grandiflorum*, large flower; *halicacabum*, unknown. All the common names make sense.

Celastrus (cel-as'trus)

bittersweet

Celastraceae

Bittersweet is just that. These woody plants have been sold for years for the beautiful fruit; unfortunately, one of the common species sold, oriental bittersweet, *Celastrus orbiculatus*, native to Japan and China, has become invasive, eating up acres of land, particularly in the Northeast and Midwest, as well as smothering our American bittersweet, *C. scandens*, which is native to eastern North America. Both are cold hardy to at least zone 4, *C. scandens* is also found in areas of zone 3.

People and nurseries have mixed them up for years; so have people trying to dig out the invader, digging out the native instead. The fact is, these are not particularly pretty plants for the home garden. True, the fruits are quite beautiful in the fall, especially as the yellow capsule splits open, revealing crimson seeds nestled in the yellow-orange interior. They are produced by the acre for the fruit by cut flower growers across the country. But the fruit is the only reason for including these plants in the home garden. The flowers are nondescript. Plants are susceptible to any number of leaf spot diseases; they are unruly scramblers and look pretty awful until in fruit in the fall. Therein lies another possible problem.

Both species are dioecious, meaning that males and females are separate (like hollies). So, if you are buying them for the fruit, which is the only sane reason to buy one, you need to buy at least two. And if you are buying two, make sure the containers are labeled as to gender. Many a gardener has waited and waited and waited for fruit to form, only to give up, because plants purchased were all males or all females. This is more prevalent in the native bittersweet; hermaphroditic forms (male not needed) are available in oriental bittersweet.

Both species can climb to 20 feet or more and, like many vines, will continue to grow as long as there is something to grow on. If you are hell-bent on having bittersweet in your garden, you may want to have it climb over a stout fence, in full sun to partial shade. But do stay away from *Celastrus orbiculatus*, if there is any chance of it escaping. Oriental bittersweet is listed as a noxious weed in five states (Connecticut, Massachusetts, New Hampshire, North Carolina, and Vermont) and is reportedly invasive in natural areas in at least sixteen others (Delaware, Illinois, Indiana, Kentucky, Maryland, Maine, Michigan, Missouri, New Jersey, New York, Pennsylania, Rhode Island, Tennessee, Virginia, Wisconsin, and West Virginia). Does not leave too many places to grow it in good conscience, does it?

I, too, have been known to get the two species confused, so I made a chart to help me when I am looking at bittersweet.

Celastrus orbiculatus. Photo by Lane Greer.

Celastrus orbiculatus	*Celastrus scandens*
Leaves round	Leaves ovate
Flowers greenish white	Flowers yellow-white
Fruit axillary, close to stems	Fruit mostly terminal, on long petioles

The easiest way to distinguish the two is leaf shape. Also, many more flowers and fruit will form on *Celastrus orbiculatus*, and its fruits are not as obvious as those of American bittersweet because they are held in the leaf axils and are often covered with the foliage; they will become visible once the foliage falls. Cultivars are available for both species, but be sure to check if it is male, female, or hermaphroditic.

Propagation
Root cuttings and softwood cuttings root reasonably quickly. Seeds may also be sown, but the gender will not be known until flowering.

Method of climbing
Plants are twiners.

Etymology
Celastrus, from *kelastros,* the Greek name for an evergreen tree; *orbiculatus,* for the rounded (orbicular) leaves; *scandens,* climbing. Bittersweet may have been a result of confusion with the unrelated bittersweet (*Solanum dulcamara*) by early colonists.

Cissus (cis′us)
grape ivy
Vitaceae

Plants of the Vitaceae are natural vines and include well-known genera such as *Ampelopsis,* porcelain vine, *Parthenocissus,* Virginia creeper, and *Vitis,* grapes. *Cissus* is best known for the ubiquitous houseplant, grape ivy, *C. rhombifolia,* which is far more at home in a mall hanging out of a container than climbing a wall. If you are in the interior landscape business, you know this plant very well; however, the genus is seldom used otherwise by gardeners.

And that is a shame, because one of the most handsome eye-catching vines I know is *Cissus discolor,* with the colorful name of rex begonia vine. It must be the gardener's aversion to annual vines that makes this such a mystery plant, because it is as colorful throughout the season as any vine I know. So the flowers are inconsequential—who needs them when a plant provides such beautiful maintenance-free foliage? In the Trial Gardens at UGA, plants grow 12 feet in a season and provide deep red angled stems with leaves painted in pink, silver, gray-green, and white above and dark red beneath. They actually seem to glow, and plants provide classy coverage of anything they are allowed to climb on or ramble through. If flowers form, which we seldom see even in zone 7, they are less than ¼ inch wide, greenish, and followed by rounded black fruit.

It is not an easy plant to find in retail outlets, but it is available online and in better garden centers and specialty nurseries.

Other species
Cissus amazonica is also a good-looking plant. It is similar in that it has handsome foliage—silver green on top and red on the bottom. The leaves are more narrow and more sharply pointed. This is even more difficult to find than *C. discolor* and not as ornamental.

Cissus discolor

Cissus discolor,
tendrils

Cissus discolor,
habit

Propagation

By semi-hardwood cuttings (i.e., not those at the tips but a few inches from the apex). Since plants are not easy to find, overwintering in a bright room is a must.

Method of climbing

Plants produce tendrils that catch on wire or thin lattice.

Etymology

Cissus, from the Greek, *kissos* ("ivy"), in reference to the climbing habit of these plants; *discolor*, of two different and usually distinct colors; *rhombifolia*, leaves diamond-shaped, rhomboidal. Rex begonia vine comes from the foliage, which reminds one of the colorful leaves of rex begonias.

Clematis (klem′a-tis)

Ranunculaceae

Entire tomes have been written about this genus. International, national, and local chapters of clematis societies exist for those who simply cannot get enough of these vines. Probably after roses (or maybe even before), they are the most popular vines in gardening. I've looked through catalogs and sites, some with more than 2,000 different taxa listed, each more beautiful than the one before.

Clematis flowers are apetalous (i.e., there are no petals), and the main color of the flower is provided by the sepals and the stamens. The fruit of many forms is as ornamental as the flower and consists of the stamens expanding and curling around, making up a ball-like feathery plume.

Unfortunately, a condition known as clematis wilt can be incredibly frustrating to gardeners. According to the International Clematis Society:

> Clematis wilt is a condition that seems to affect the large-flowered, spring-blooming clematis more than other varieties. It is characterized by a complete collapse of either the entire plant, just one of the shoots, or just part of a shoot. It will hit a healthy-looking plant overnight and will look as though the plant was being starved for water. With clematis wilt, however, the plant has plenty of water and is loaded with flower buds that are about to open. What a disappointment! One must not confuse the dying off of lower leaves in the heat of the summer with wilt. The growing tip will become very limp with the wilt.

This and other societies and their sites should be visited and supported, but

Clematis armandii 'Apple Blossom'

appear in early spring is what most gardeners keen for. The buds appear as early as February, and the five-sepaled flowers open a few weeks later. If the weather stays cool, flowering persists for two to four weeks.

Drought, sunburn, and other related stresses can result in entire sections of the plant going brown and dying back. However, all in all, it is a terrific plant, providing months of satisfaction.

'Apple Blossom' has flower buds that are blushed pink. When the flowers open, they appear to be the same as the species unless you look at the undersides: there the blush will be apparent.

'Snowdrift' is similar to the species but has larger flowers (2 to 2½ inches across).

Clematis cirrhosa (sir-o′sa)

winter clematis

zones 7–9

I often find clematis similar to orchids: they are pretty ugly when not in flower. This species does not have that problem, simply because it actually goes dormant most of the time when it is not flowering. Plants will go dormant in the summer, start growing in the fall, flower in the winter and very early spring, and go dormant again as temperatures rise.

Clematis cirrhosa

Clematis cirrhosa
'Freckles'

The simple, often three-lobed leaves are dark glossy green, a characteristic that makes the foliage stand apart from other clematis. The nodding cream-colored flowers occur singly or in a few-flowered inflorescence and are 1 to 1½ inches across, often with fine silky hairs. The fruit is made up of the slender styles and is quite handsome and persistent.

I have seen outstanding plants in English gardens and some nice examples on the West Coast of Canada and the United States, where, in a sunny location, they can be quite vigorous. In marginal areas, however, they may be frustratingly slow, and a good hard winter may make them toast. In my north Georgia garden, they did well for a couple of years, but flowering was sparse, likely because of the shady conditions. Plants retired after three years.

var. *balearica* is quite common, bearing larger flowers with some maroon spotting within the flower.

'Freckles' is easily found in good nurseries and is likely a selection of the variety above. Similar large flowers (approximately 2 inches across), but heavily spotted or flecked with maroon to violet, and borne on long flower stems.

'Wisley Cream' is an old-fashioned selection, similar to the species, with simple, light green leaves and creamy flowers.

Clematis montana (mon-tan'a)
anemone clematis

zones 6–9

A native of China, this plant is a grower! I have seen it reach heights of 50 to 60 feet clambering up trees, and at least 20 feet over pergolas and arbors. Plants have small (1 to 1½ inches wide) white flowers that can cover the plant in spring and early summer. The fragrance can be quite delicious, reminding one of vanilla. They require lots of space or lots of cutting back so they won't take over the world. They don't reseed like the pesky *Clematis terniflora*; they are simply rampant—vigorous and hungry. The following quote nicely sums up the feelings of many: "I've tried several times to get completely rid of the climber *Clematis montana* growing along the fence. . . . It smothers one of the flowering cherry trees, and is generally a nuisance—but it still lives! And I still quite like it!" (mooseyscountrygarden.com). They have many fans, who like these bodacious plants with their lacey leaves and attitude. But to be honest, it is the varieties and selections with *C. montana* as a parent (referred to as the Montana Group) that people are falling in love with, even though they also are vigorous.

Clematis montana. Photo by Suzy Bales.

'Brewster' is relatively new (1989) and is characterized by large pale pink and rose-colored flowers. Introduced by clematis guru Brewster Rogerson.

'Broughton Star' always intrigued me with its single and occasionally semi-double flowers on somewhat less vigorous stems. However, when I saw it growing in the town of Sterling, Tasmania, I was blown away. It was absolutely covered in rose-colored flowers and well behaved.

Clematis montana 'Broughton Star'

Clematis montana
'Freda'

Clematis montana
'Grandiflora'

'Elizabeth' has been a favorite for years, bearing nicely scented light pink flowers on 20- to 30-foot stems.

'Freda', introduced in 1985, is still not very common in the United States. The small pink sepals are characterized by a darker rose-colored margin.

'Grandiflora' has larger flowers (up to 3 inches across) than the species; a clean wonderful white, they cover the vine in the spring. Exquisite.

'Mayleen' has medium pink flowers with contrasting handsome yellow stamens on deep green foliage.

'Rubens' is another longtime favorite of clematis lovers. It has been around since 1886, so it has had a chance to impress many generations of gardeners. The soft pink flowers are about 2½ to 3 inches wide and abundantly produced on vigorous plants. Unfortunately, perhaps due to its longevity, there is a great deal of variability in flower power and vigor. However, if dealing with a specialist nursery, a good 'Rubens' is a winner, albeit with some ruthless cutbacks if it gets out of hand.

Clematis montana 'Rubens'

Clematis tangutica (tan-gute′i-ka)
orange peel clematis
zones 5–9

These vigorous plants bear pendulous blooms consisting of thick yellow sepals (like orange peels). The flowers are relatively small but are followed by some of the most wonderful persistent fluffy fruit. They remind me of some of those fluffy made-up little Shih Tzus at the Westminster Dog Show. I have had problems with wilt in north Georgia but have seen beautiful aggressive plants in Niagara Falls. The cultivars and hybrids fall under the Tangutica Group.

'Bill MacKenzie' has large (2-inch-long) bright yellow flowers from early to late summer, followed by beautiful silky seedheads in autumn. In the Armitage garden, plants were lovely but wilted out on me.

'Helios' was introduced as a shorter, better-behaved tangutica than others in the group and more useful for a smaller garden. Plants were bred, probably from *Clematis tangutica* and *C.* 'Golden Harvest' in 1988 by the Boskoop Research Station in the Netherlands. Vines grow 6 to 8 feet tall with yellow sepals and purple stamens, followed by the handsome fruit.

'Lambton Park' is similar to other cultivars to my uneducated eye.

*Clematis
tangutica*

Clematis terniflora (tern-i-flor'a)

sweet autumn clematis

zones 5–9

This beautiful Chinese species has many admirers as well as an equal number of detractors. I guess it is fair to say that plants are so easy to grow and so reliable that they seem to be a good choice for beginning gardeners and those who see it in full white dress in the fall. I was one of those. It is easy to agree that the handsome foliage (sometimes with silver chevrons) and the seemingly endless number of flowers are hard not to love.

For the rest of us, however, it is a terrible pest, reseeding everywhere and popping up wherever the seeds are blown. In the spring, seedlings emerge to climb through hollies and spireas, often in shaded areas, where they simply will not look good. Gardeners are always optimistic and feel that maybe a nice clematis prancing through a boring buddleia is a good idea. It is not. I too was one of those.

By all means, love them, but I suggest the love should be in someone else's garden. There are so many beautiful clematis, why mess with a potential dandelion? If you need fall flowers, try anemones and asters.

Clematis terniflora

Clematis texensis (tex-en'sis)

Texas clematis

zones 5–9

This is probably my favorite group of clematis. No doubt I am biased because of the success I have had with some of the cultivars compared to large-flowered hybrids. There is nothing particularly remarkable about the foliage, nor are the flowers the biggest or the brightest. For me, however, they are almost idiot-proof—scrambling through shrubs or growing up fences and pergolas. The species is little known, which is a shame. It produces small urn-shaped red flowers whose sepals are turned up at the ends. The fruits are relatively large and persistent. However, the species is a slow grower, shy of flowering, and in the eyes of many is less showy than some of the more popular cultivars in the Texensis stable.

The cultivars and hybrids with *Clematis texensis* in the blood (referred to as Texensis Group) are vigorous growers, easily scaling 20 feet in a season. The flowers are always deep pink to scarlet, regardless of cultivar, and the fruits, like those of the species, are large and persistent. Plants need full sun and have few problems with heat and humidity.

'Catherine Clanwilliam' is a relatively new selection with wide-open rosy pink flowers. The tips of the sepals are recurved.

'Duchess of Albany' has been around forever it seems, actually only since 1890. However, its unsurpassed garden performance will keep it around for many years to come. The tulip-shaped flowers of pink and muted red occur abundantly in the spring and occasionally in the summer and fall. The fruits are persistent.

'Étoile Rose' has nodding bell-shaped flowers, dark rose usually with a silver-pink margin.

'Gravetye Beauty' is a hybrid with *Clematis texensis* and our native *C. viorna*. Plants grow only about 6 feet tall and produce dark red flowers with thin sepals.

'Princess Diana' was released in 1984 and is a cross of *Clematis texensis* with *C.* 'Bees' Jubilee'. I love the larger flowers and the deeper red compared to 'Duchess of Albany', but for me, the "duchess" is still the best performer. (Both make it into Lyndy Broder's Top Ten list, which see).

'Sir Trevor Lawrence' (*Clematis texensis* × *C.* 'Star of India') produces the same tulip-shaped red flowers seen in all these selections. Plants grow 8 to 12 feet tall.

Clematis texensis.
Photo by Donnie Carlson.

Clematis texensis
'Princess Diana'

Clematis texensis
'Duchess of Albany'

Other clematis

I have listed a few species and cultivars that I enjoy, but it is impossible not to be impressed with the descriptions and photos of the hundreds of other clematis hybrids found in catalogs and online. A beginner or a gardener with little experience in clematis is quickly confused with terminology, species, maintenance, and other issues, often saying, "I'll just buy what is for sale down the road." To provide a little help for us non-clematisers, I have provided two lists.

Clematis for beginning gardeners

Compiled by members of the International Clematis Society (www.clematisinternational.com), this list provides cultivars from various groupings that are easy to grow and relatively resistant to diseases such as clematis wilt. I have included only a sampling of their choices; go online for all of them. Remember, however, that they have been selected by members all over the world and may not be the best plant for your climate. No list ever will fit everyone.

Small-flowered clematis
Early flowering: Alpinas and macropetalas: 'Frankie', 'Markham's Pink', 'Pamela Jackson', 'White Swan'
Montana Group: 'Broughton Star', 'Grandiflora', 'Mayleen'
Viticella Group: 'Abundance', 'Betty Corning', 'Étoile Violette', 'Madame Julia Correvon', 'Walenburg'
Late flowering: Tangutica Group: 'Bill MacKenzie', 'Helios'
Texensis Group: 'Duchess of Albany', 'Princess Diana'

Large-flowered clematis
Early flowering: 'General Sikorski', 'Guernsey Cream', 'Mrs. George Jackson', 'Niobe', 'Warszawska Nike'
Late flowering: Blue Angel (= 'Blekitny Aniol'), 'Gipsy Queen', 'Huldine', 'Jackmanii', 'Polish Spirit', 'Ramona'

Lyndy Broder's Top Ten clematis

Lyndy sits on the board of directors of the International Clematis Society and is a frequent contributor to their Web site. She has attended workshops in the United States, England, Poland, Estonia, Finland, Sweden, and Japan, all for the love of clematis. Here are her choices for the best and easiest clematis and her reasons why. You will notice that nos. 2 thru 6 earn double points, being both on her list and the previous list. Says Lyndy:

1. 'Arabella'. I love this clematis so much that when a big box store carried it, I bought a whole flat and used it as a groundcover edging a large

mixed shrub border. Small flowers (3 to 3.5 inches) open a medium purplish blue with yellow stamens and fade to a very pale blue with whitish
stamens as the pollen disappears, creating a stunning display of a multi-
tude of star-shaped shades of blue. The longest blooming clematis in my
garden, starting in early April and ceasing at frost.

2. 'Betty Corning'. Should be in every American garden: its parentage includes our native *Clematis crispa*, which imbues it with a sweet

Clematis
'Guernsey
Cream'

Clematis 'Niobe'

Clematis 'Arabella'.
Photo by Lyndy Broder.

Clematis 'Arabella' and oakleaf hydrangea. Photo by Lyndy Broder.

Clematis 'Betty Corning'. Photo by Lyndy Broder.

Clematis texensis 'Duchess of Albany'. Photo by Lyndy Broder.

fragrance sometimes described as reminiscent of tangerines. The scent is especially pleasing on a cool evening. This pale blue clematis displays hundreds of small (2-inch) bell-shaped flowers with recurved tips and a white cross inside the base.

3. 'Duchess of Albany' is the most floriferous texensis in my garden. This charmer combines a deep rose pink middle bar surrounded by lilac pink margins on 2-inch sepals that are slightly recurved, displaying a sharp tip. The seedheads are a significant asset as the vine appears to be covered in hundreds of golden pinwheels. Any deadheading will help to encourage further blooms, but those seedheads are a sight to behold.

4. 'Princess Diana' has the most luminous deep pink blooms I have ever seen. The first time I saw this plant was in a walled Irish garden where its iridescent bloom outshone all other flora and beckoned me to come closer. In my garden it has the same effect on visitors. As with all texensis, it blooms on new wood, therefore pruning in early spring is suggested. The quickest way to kill a texensis is to have poor drainage.

5. 'Étoile Violette' is probably the most common purple clematis next to the ubiquitous *Clematis* 'Jackmanii'. It, however, is the preferred selection because it is mildew resistant. This dark purple flower has characteristic chartreuse stamens, creating a nice contrast. You can prune at any time to bring it back into shape.

Clematis texensis 'Princess Diana'. Photo by Meg Green.

6. 'Madame Julia Correvon' brings a luscious rich purplish red to your garden, glorious against the deep green of a yew. The blooms are 3 inches, somewhat gappy with the sepals slightly twisting as it matures. This deep color does best in full sun or partial shade.

7. 'Venosa Violacea' has one of the most intriguing colorations of the viticellas: a white base color infused with dark purple veins, which merge to solid purple margins. The blackish

Clematis
'Madame Julia
Correvon' and
hydrangea.
Photo by Lyndy
Broder.

Clematis 'Venosa
Violacea'

purple anthers with whitish pollen complete the delicate combination. The variations in individual flowers are fascinating. The blooms are up to 5 inches across.

8. 'Rooguchi' (a cross between *Clematis integrifolia* and our native *C. reticulata*) was bred a mere twenty years ago as a distinctive single flower used in the cut flower trade in Japan for tea ceremony flower arrangements. Imagine iridescent shades of purplish blues and deep plums on four heavily ridged sepals, which form a 2-inch straight narrow bell, which slightly recurves at the tip. Then take this single bell (as it is used in flower arrangements), multiply it by a hundred, and place where the evening sun backlights its shimmery glow. A fabulous garden plant, especially in hot, humid environments.

9. Pink Champagne (= 'Kakio') is an early bloomer, with flowers so beautiful that this is the type most nurseries sell. The large flowers (6 inches) have vivid purplish pink sepals that glow while becoming lighter toward the center of the sepals; the pale yellow anthers viewed from the side give the appearance of a lighted birthday cake. I have grown this for twenty years, and I stop every time I go by to admire the combination.

10. Josephine (= 'Evijohill'). A delightful true double clematis, which slowly unfolds her sepals over time, so that on the vine you will have some

Clematis Pink
Champagne (= 'Kakio').
Photo by Lyndy Broder.

Clematis
'Rooguchi'. Photo
by Lyndy Broder

flowers that have the large sepals open with a very tight center, combined with other flowers that look like a full pom-pom. The blooms are 4 to 5 inches across with lilac-pink sepals marked with a deep pink central bar. This clematis only needs to be tidied up in the late winter with minimal pruning to a strong node."

Thank you, Lyndy. Again, this is only a smattering of available and wonderful clematis for the garden. Clematis plants are available in almost every plant store in the country, and for those cultivars you must have but cannot find locally, there are many Web sites that provide information and the plants themselves. Happy hunting.

Clematis Josephine (= 'Evijohill'). Photo by Lyndy Broder.

Propagation
By semi-hardwood cuttings, i.e., not those at the tips but a few inches from the apex.

Method of climbing
Plants hold on by the twining petioles. They are self-climbers for the most part.

Etymology
Clematis, from the Greek, *klēmatis*, for various climbing plants; *alpina*, alpine, from high mountains; *armandii*, in honor of French missionary Armand David (1826–1900); *cirrhosa*, with tendrils; *macropetala*, large flowers; *montana*, pertaining to mountains; *tangutica*, named for the Tangut people of northwest China; *terniflora*, flowers in threes; *texensis*, of Texas; *viticella*, vinelike.

Clerodendrum (kler-o-den'drum)

glorybower

Verbenacaeae

This is a most diverse genus, including small trees and shrubs like harlequin glorybower, *Clerodendrum trichotomum*, and rose glorybower, *C. bungei*, annuals such as blue glorybower, *C. ugandense*, and greenhouse plants like bleeding heart vine, *C. thompsoniae*, as well as a number of handsome vines, my favorite being *C. splendens*.

Clerodendrum splendens (splen'dens)

glorybower vine

zones 9–11

The opposite, deep green lustrous leaves are ovate with a pointed tip and smooth margins. The plant develops slowly in temperate climates and will likely not grow more than 6 to 10 feet in height. However, the spectacular flowers, which do not open until very late summer or fall, are well worth the wait. The flowers are arranged in a many-flowered inflorescence that is formed in the axils. They are 55 mph flowers but are even better when enjoyed close up. Their color is eye-catching due to the lighter red sepals and the brilliantly scarlet petals, with the four long, extended stamens appearing to escape, and the pistil arching down from the flowers.

Clerodendrum splendens. Photo by Meg Green.

Propagation

Seeds, or by softwood cuttings in the summer. Root in sand with bottom heat.

Method of climbing

Stems twine around supports. A little help to get the plants started is useful, but once started, plants are self-climbers.

Etymology

Clerodendrum, from the Greek, *klēros* ("chance") and *dendron* ("tree"), from their supposed medicinal qualities; *splendens*, splendid. Glorybower, from the glorious flowers and the habit of growing in a shady, sheltered place.

Clitoria (kli-tor′ee-a)
butterfly pea
Papilionaceae

There are many species in this genus, but only *Clitoria ternatea*, blue pea, is seen in North American gardens. This plant is an annual in most climes, but as with other wonderful long-flowering vines in this book, who cares? The more I grow it, the more it grows on me. It is vigorous, easy to grow, produces purple-blue flowers most of the season, and can hide even ugly cement walls. What's more, its name is always a conversation maker, or a mumble maker. For example, when the professor discusses this plant while trying to keep the attention of a group of high school kids, it can be a little awkward. But no worse than *Lobelia siphilitica* or the favorite among students, nipplefruit (*Solanum mammosum*). Mumble makers, for sure, every one of them.

Butterfly pea consists of smooth compound leaves, 3 to 4 inches long, with five to seven ovate leaflets. The royal blue flowers are borne in the axils and have the standard pea-flower look, with five petals, one being the larger "keel" and others below and beneath it. Flowers persist for a week or so, but additional flowers are formed all summer. Plants can carry more than a dozen open flowers at any one time. The oblong fruit, like a pea pod, is also persistent.

Plants are popular among people in Singapore, Malaysia, and Thailand, where blue food coloring, often used in traditional rice cakes and desserts, is extracted from the flowers. A number of naturally occurring variants may occur, such as light blue, dark blue, purple, and even white flowers. They will not all come true from seed, but differences from the species will be found.

'Blue Sails' has semi-double deep blue flowers.

Clitoria ternatea

Clitoria ternatea,
dark blue flowers.
Photo by Meg Green.

Clitoria ternatea,
light blue flowers.
Photo by Meg Green.

Propagation

Collect seeds from plants anytime in the summer and fall, and replant after all threat of frost has passed.

Method of climbing

Stems twine around supports. A little help to get the plants started is useful, but once started, plants are self-climbers.

Etymology

Clitoria, Linnaeus thought the flower was suggestive of the clitoris; *ternatea*, of the island of Ternate in the Moluccas. Butterfly pea, likely from the pea-like flowers, which are attractive to many species of butterflies.

Cobaea (ko-bay'a)
missionary bells
Polemoniaceae

Cup and saucer vine (*Cobaea scandens*) is not as popular as it was just ten years ago. Perhaps this is true of many annual vines in that they have been overshadowed by more colorful annuals and perennials. Regardless, I always recommend this to gardeners looking for an easy vine for privacy and ornamental value.

These Mexican natives can grow 20 feet in a single season producing compound leaves with four to six oblong leaflets per leaf. The flowers buds are erect and held on long (6- to 10-inch) flower stems but the open flowers are horizontal and easy to gaze upon. They consist of large sepals (saucer) and open cup-like petals. When first open, the flowers are creamy green, but as they age, the flowers turn violet to deep purple with a subtle honey scent. There are a few oddities, like those with variegated petals, and a white-flowered form (var. *alba*) as well.

Cobaea scandens. Photo by Meg Green

Plants are easy to grow, even for children, and have wonderful full-bodied flowers. Vines can cover arbors and pergolas or grow through other plants. Unfortunately, they don't flower well until late summer if the seeds are started outside. If they can be propagated indoors under lights, they will mature faster outdoors and flower earlier.

Propagation

By semi-hardwood terminal cuttings or by seeds. Seeds are by far the easiest. They may be collected or purchased. Soak overnight and start about four weeks before plants are to be put in the garden. Otherwise, seeds may be sown in situ after the threat of frost has passed. Sowing in the ground early will not accomplish anything.

Method of climbing

Plants are self-climbers by tendrils at the nodes.

Etymology

Cobaea, named in honor of Bernardo Cobo (1572–1659), a Spanish Jesuit missionary in Mexico and Peru; *scandens*, climbing. Cup and saucer vine, from the similarity to a cup resting in a saucer; missionary bells, likely from the bell-shaped flowers that were undoubtedly planted around missions and other religious areas.

Cobaea scandens var. *alba* at Sissinghurst

Codonopsis (ko-don-op'sis)

bonnet bellflower
Campanulaceae

This is a poorly used and seldom seen genus in American gardens, which is truly a shame. Reasons for its absence vary, but lack of availability, poor heat tolerance, and subtle rather than bright-colored nodding flowers are surely among them. Having stated the negatives, I hasten to add that the flowers are quite wonderful and some species are cold hardy to about zone 4. The flowers can be cream-colored or light blue to violet-blue, but many have beautiful markings within the flower as well. Of the thirty species, the best known is probably *Codonopsis ovata*, a 2-foot-tall perennial. A number of species are climbers, but only a few are useful as vines for most North American gardens. All need well-drained soils and tolerate partial shade to full sun.

Codonopsis convolvulacea (kon-vol-vew-lay′ see-a)
climbing bonnet bellflower
zones 4–8

Plants grow from a swollen rhizome, and the smooth thin stems bear alternate 2-inch-long, lanceolate leaves, often with a heart-shaped base. The stems grow to about 10 feet in length and are best sited to allow them to scramble through shrubs rather than growing up a structure. The solitary campanula-like flowers are characterized by having five distinct petal lobes and are usually azure to dark blue. There is a white form ('Alba').

Native to southwest China and the Himalayas, plants tolerate reasonably cold temperatures but are poor choices for heat and humidity.

Other species
Codonopsis clematidea is a branching, sprawling plant, not sure if it wants to be a climber or a sprawling weed. The flowers are subtly beautiful, quite pale blue on the outside with tangerine and black markings within. They grow only about 3 feet tall. Cold hardy to about zone 4.

Codonopsis tangshen, dang shen, is a twining plant with 6-foot-tall long stems and solitary yellow to chartreuse green flowers with netted and spotted purple markings at the base within. Plants are used in Chinese medicine; the root is widely used as a substitute for ginseng, for increased energy and other positive outcomes. It is often cooked with rice.

Propagation
By seeds or division of the rhizome. Plant seeds indoors under lights until plants are large enough to place outdoors.

Method of climbing
Plants are sprawlers. Stems will also twine around each other but are not considered to be self-climbers.

Etymology
Codonopsis, from the Greek, *kōdōn* ("bell") and *ŏpsis* ("looks like"), referring to the bell-shaped flowers; *clematidea*, like clematis; *convolvulacea*, similar to *Convolvulus*. Bonnet bellflower, not sure about the bonnet, but most plants in this family are referred to as bellflowers.

Cucurbita (kew-ker'bi-ta)
gourd, squash
Cucurbitaceae

The cucumber family is seldom thought of as ornamental vines, but vines many of them are, and ornamental is in the eyes of the beholder. One of the main genera in the family is *Cucumis*, which includes cucumbers (*C. sativus*) and cantaloupes and melons (*C. melo*), in all their shapes and colors. The other vining genus is *Cucurbita*, similar to be sure and a catchall for some other melons and vegetables like pumpkin and everyone's favorite, zucchini. However, as far as ornamental vines are concerned, this genus is also the place for some of the weirdest of the weird, the wild and wacky gourds.

Unlike their vegetable relatives, gourds are mainly grown for ornament. All are tendril-bearing vines that will sprawl if not supported. There are wonderful shapes and colors, small and large gourds that anyone can grow just for the hell of it. I have no idea where to start, but one thing I do know is that unless you are selling these things for a living, one should never be serious when growing gourds—these are a blast. Types of gourds include turban gourds, ball gourds, egg gourds, oddities like orange-warted and small spoon gourds, and probably a dozen more. Some are subspecies of *Cucurbita pepo* (ssp. *ovifera*); others may be classified as *C. moschata*, *C. maxima*, or *C. ficifolia*. One of the best sites I have found describing the different gourds and edible cucurbits is Wayne's Word (http://waynesword.palomar.edu/ww0503.htm#fruit).

Cucurbita pepo, flower. Photo by Meg Green.

Cucurbita pepo, fruit. Photo by Meg Green.

All gourd plants are self-climbing by tendrils and generally produce large heart-shaped leaves quite useful for shading an arbor or screening unpleasant sights. The large yellow flowers look like cucumber flowers, but depending on the variety, the fruit will differ. All plants are monoecious, meaning that separate male and female flowers occur on the same plant. If fruit production appears to be a problem (i.e., female flowers fall off with no hint of fruit) then simply take a mature male flower (one with pollen), strip back the petals, and use it like a paintbrush to pollinate the females. If you are not sure which ones are female, pollinate as many as you can. You will be tired of the fruit before long.

For those who wish to cure gourds, a few hints follow. The first phase is the surface drying, which is accomplished under room temperature in a dark, well-ventilated place. The skin will harden, and the color will be set. This takes about a week. Check gourds every day, and discard those that go soft or show decay or mold. The second phase is internal drying, and this can take up to six weeks. Any surface mold can be wiped off, but if the fruit decays or becomes shriveled, discard it. The curing process is finished when the gourd is very light and the seeds reverberate within. Cured gourds can be painted, waxed, drilled, sculpted, or otherwise defaced.

Lagenaria is another genus of gourds, similar in habit but with white flowers. My favorite is *Lagenaria siceraria* (bottle gourd, dinosaur gourd), which can reach 30 feet in height with oval to kidney-shaped leaves. The fruit varies in length, from 3 inches to 3 feet, and may be shaped like a bottle, club, dipper, or dumbbell. Plants are also known as calabash and white-flowered gourd. Even one is quite a handful for my favorite neighbor (see back cover).

You have to love gourds. They are fun, fascinating, easy to grow, and require no reasons why. The downsides may be when they cover your house, which they surely will, or when you have to do something with the fruit. After all, there are only so many bird houses that are needed.

Propagation
By seeds, in the home. Plant out after all threat of frost has passed and the ground has warmed up. Planting in situ in cold soil results in rotting seeds.

Method of climbing
Plants climb by tendrils. Provide something the tendrils can clasp, and they will climb to the heavens.

Etymology
Cucurbita, a Latin name for a gourd; *moschata*, musky; *pepo*, a specialized berry with a hard and very thick exocarp or rind.

Dalechampia (doll-shamp' ee-a)
purple wings
Euphorbiaceae

I grew bow tie vine (*Dalechampia dioscoreifolia*) in the Trial Gardens at UGA for a number of years, and it was so fascinating that everyone commented on it. I was quite proud of myself for including such a rare gem, until I walked into the Niagara Parks Butterfly Conservatory in Niagara Falls, Ontario, and saw plant after plant growing in baskets in the greenhouse. It turns out that *Dalechampia* is a primary food source for the gray cracker butterfly, and by the time the larvae were finished dining, there was little about its ornamental features to extol.

Larvae aside, I still think this is a really neat plant, rapidly growing 10 to 12 feet in height. There is nothing exciting, however, about the alternate, simple 6-inch lanceolate leaves that are pointed at the end and somewhat heart-shaped at the base. Nor is there anything exciting about the small yellow flowers that appear once the plant becomes mature. The exciting part of the plant is the two large rose-pink bracts, each 2½ to 3 inches long, on either side of the flowers, giving the whole thing an appearance of a rosy bow tie. The bracts are distinctly nerved and toothed and without doubt people will comment on this wonderful floral arrangement.

It is probably a better conservatory plant than a garden plant in much of the country, because it takes until at least late summer, even in zone 7, to see any flowers. I have never seen

Dalechampia dioscoreifolia, flowers. Photo by Meg Green.

Dalechampia dioscoreifolia. Photo by Alan Shapiro.

a plant smothered with flowers, but it takes only a few to make quite a show. In colder zones, there may be insufficient time or heat for flowers to form.

Plants are native to Mexico and should be treated as an annual in all but frost-free environments.

Propagation
By seed, or by semi-hardwood cuttings. Use bottom heat (72F) and mist for best rooting.

Method of climbing
Plants produce large twining stems. They should be trained and tied when the stems are first produced, and even as they mature, to produce the best effect.

Etymology
Dalechampia, named for French physician and botanist Jacques Dalechamps (1513–1588); *dioscoreifolia*, from *dioscorea* ("yam") and *folia* ("leaves"), the leaves resemble those of yams. Bow tie vine, as mentioned above; purple wings because the large bracts have the appearance of wings, particularly when the wind is blowing.

Decumaria (dek-ew-mar'ee-a)
climbing hydrangea
Hydrangeaceae

Climbing hydrangeas have a lot of company. In this book, I have listed three of them, all sufficiently similar to have earned the same common name, but different enough to be placed in different genera (the other two are *Hydrangea* and *Schizophragma*).

Decumaria barbara is native to the southeastern United States and will climb to 30 feet, but half that height is more common. Plants bear opposite ovate to oblong leaves, which in itself is no big deal, but they are shiny, lustrous, and glossy, enough to notice them even when not in flower. This is the best characteristic of the plant, other than its name of wood vamp (love that name). The tiny pale white flowers are sweetly fragrant and are held in a many-flowered slightly domed terminal cluster about 2 to 3 inches wide. All flowers are fertile, making for a rather bland display. That they have no sterile flowers makes them easy to tell from *Hydrangea* and *Schizophragma*, both of which have sterile flowers in the inflorescence. It is the sterile flowers (that look like the bracts of a dogwood) that provide the ornamental value to those other genera.

Plants are deciduous; they can be found under shady canopies but will tolerate bright light in the garden. Plants can be used as a groundcover but will flower only when climbing. This is a good plant for climbing a wall, as it has adhesive pads to help it climb. A number of cultivars (including 'Margaret' and 'Vickie') are offered, perhaps with more glossy leaves, but I haven't detected many differences. Prune when necessary; flowers are formed on new wood. Plants are best for zones 7–9.

Another species occasionally offered is Chinese climbing hydrangea, *Decumaria sinensis*, whose leaves are more rounded and not as shiny; the flower cluster is flat-topped, and the flowers have a musky smell. Plants, however, are evergreen. Still, there is little sense in buying this one when our native works equally well or better. Hardiness is a guess—perhaps a little less hardy than the native.

Propagation
By semi-hardwood cuttings in a mist bed and bottom heat.

Method of climbing
Plants climb with self-adhesive aerial rootlets, difficult to take down once established.

Etymology
Decumaria, from the Latin, *decimus* ("ten"), for the number of parts of the flower; *barbara*, foreign; *sinensis*, of China.

Decumaria barbara, fertile flowers

Decumaria barbara

Dicentra (die-sen'tra)
bleeding heart
Fumariaceae

When I told people I had brought a climbing yellow bleeding heart home from a plant trip in Europe, most listeners thought I was crazy, lying, or senile. Whoever heard of a yellow bleeding heart, much less one that climbed?

Dicentra scandens is a fabulous vine, one that produces many stems in spring and bears small, alternate leaves with many small leaflets. The yellow flowers are produced in many-flowered racemes; the first flowers open in early summer, and flowering continues all season. Plants are cold hardy to about zone 7b; however, they don't seem to persist very long in Raleigh, North Carolina, zone 7a. In the Trial Gardens at UGA (zone 7b), plants die back to the ground in the winter to return with a dozen new stems in the spring. Plants routinely grow 10 feet in a single season. My colleague Linda Copeland took some home, and it grows through and over her foundation plants, leading her to tear it out at times. Plants perform best in partial shade but can tolerate more sun than normal bleeding hearts.

Its lack of cold hardiness can be frustrating, but the other drawback I notice is that as the flowers ripen, they begin to turn black at the base. This results in a mixture of the new, beautifully golden flowers and the over-mature flowers on the same vine. Not awful, but sometimes a little distracting.

Dicentra scandens 'Athens Yellow'

'Athens Yellow' resulted from the plant I brought back, selected for more golden flowers and rapid vigorous growth. Today it is mixed up with the species and difficult to tell apart.

Propagation
By semi-hardwood cuttings. Use bottom heat (72F) and mist for best rooting. I have seen reports of propagation by seed; if you can find some, give them a go. My plants seldom bear fruit or seed.

Method of climbing
The terminal leaflet acts as a tendril, and plants are self-climbers. They can climb through wire or other thin support. They also sprawl and clamber through many shrubs.

Etymology
Dicentra, from the Greek, *dis* ("twice") and *kentron* ("spur"), for the spurs on the flowers; *scandens*, climbing.

Dicentra scandens 'Athens Yellow', flowers

Dioscorea (dye-os-kor′ee-a)
yam
Dioscoreaceae

Bring one species of this genus, air potato (*Dioscorea bulbifera*), into the garden, and you invite many comments—some positive, some negative—along with it. The broadly heart-shaped, obviously veined leaves are up to 8 inches long and are quite handsome. The plants are vigorous and cover large pergolas or arbors without trouble. The positive comments come from observing the aerial potato-like tubers, located in the leaf axils, that arise from small spikes of greenish flowers. The flowers are either male or female (dioecious). These are replaced by ovoid warty "potatoes" (actually bulbils) that are whitish to tan and range in size from a golf ball to a softball. The bulbils are fun to look at, the vines grow quickly, and the leaves are most handsome, especially when the sun is behind them. We place it on an arbor that people walk under to get into the garden. Great fun to look up and see Mr. Potato Head smiling down at you.

Plants are annuals to be sure, but the potatoes produced that fall can produce new plants the next season. We have grown this plant in the Trial Gardens at UGA for years; sometimes it returns, sometimes it doesn't, and it has not been a pest, yet!

Dioscorea bulbifera,
backlit foliage

Dioscorea bulbifera,
"potatoes"

However, the potential to be invasive may bring on a flurry of negative comments. This species is listed as an invasive in many southeastern states, forming dense masses of vines that cover and kill native vegetation, including trees, in forest edges and disturbed areas. It is a potential problem in frost-free areas, but most gardeners should not be concerned that it will become invasive in, say, Oberlin, Ohio.

Other species in the genus are true yams (*Dioscorea rotunda, D. cayenensis, D. alata*), not to be confused with the sweet potato, which is in an entirely different family (Convolvulaceae) and an entirely different genus (*Ipomoea*). Yams are underground tubers and don't produce edible aerial structures. The air potato is a common food crop throughout most tropical regions of the world and was introduced from Africa for food and medicinal purposes in the early 1900s.

Propagation
By the aerial bulbils. Plant in a container, allowing a third of the bulbil to be above the surface. Water sparingly until new growth appears. Grow in warm (approximately 70F) temperatures.

Method of climbing
By twining stems.

Etymology

Dioscorea, named in honor of Pedanios Dioscorides, first-century Greek physician and herbalist; *bulbifera*, bulb-bearing, often used for plants whose flowers are replaced with bulbils.

Eccremocarpus (ek-rem-o-kar′pus)
Chilean glory flower
Bignoniaceae

Five species of herbaceous tropical vines occur in the genus, and it is reasonably popular on the West Coast. Plants are native to Chile and Peru and are considered annuals in much of this country. The most common species is *Eccremocarpus scaber* and likely the only one gardeners will be able to find.

Plants bear angled stems, from which the somewhat rough, opposite, compound, 2- to 3-inch-long leaves are borne. Under optimal conditions, I have seen plants grow 10 to 15 feet tall; unfortunately I have also seen 2- to 3-inch-tall plants struggling to throw out a few flowers. The common name of the genus suggests something glorious, and when dozens of 1-inch-long brightly colored tubular flowers occur on the plants, it is quite eye-catching; however, I save "glorious" for the stars in a clear northern sky, and this doesn't even come close to reaching those heights. The red-orange flowers are tipped with yellow and are produced in 4- to 6-inch-long inflorescences. Plants are useful for walls but are better to grow through shrubs or over fences.

Eccremocarpus scaber. Photo by Suzy Bales.

I have read reports from gardeners that suggest plants will survive short periods of temperatures into the low 20s, but a ton of mulch would be necessary if cold temperatures persist.

Cultivars are similar in habit and vigor to the species. The Anglia hybrids offer flowers in various colors: 'Aureus' bears golden-yellow flowers, 'Carmineus' is carmine-red, 'Roseus' has pink flowers. Tresco hybrids, from the Isles of Scilly, provide flowers in salmon, cream, crimson, and as a mix.

Propagation

Plants are essentially always propagated by seed. Plants flower the first season from seed. Sow in the winter indoors under high light conditions, and place in garden when all danger of frost is past. Occasionally some of the single-colored cultivars are multiplied by semi-hardwood cuttings.

Method of climbing

Plants produce tendrils, allowing it to be a self-climber.

Etymology

Eccremocarpus, from the Greek, *ĕkkrĕmĕs* ("hanging") and *karpos* ("fruit"), referring to the thin, pendulous pod; *scabra*, rough, referring to somewhat roughly hairy leaves.

Ficus (fie′cus)
fig
Moraceae

I am drinking coffee at five o'clock in the morning, working on this silly book, and remembering how I used to relish Fig Newtons as a kid. Now here I am writing about them. Edible figs (*Ficus carica*) probably were grown from at least 2700 B.C. in southwest Asia and are still widely grown today, including in California. If you aren't into Fig Newtons, then perhaps, like me, you have tortured a weeping fig, *F. benjamina*, in the home or dorm room, or admired rubber plant, *F. elastica*, in the mall or office. It may be no surprise to learn that over 800 species of fig are known, mostly from the tropics or subtropics. During a visit to the wonderful Daintree Discovery Centre, near Cairns, Australia, I was able to admire hundreds of the huge fig trees with small yellow fruit that grow throughout tropical rainforests in northeastern Queensland. The Daintree Rainforest, listed as a World Heritage Site, is among the most ancient ecosystems on earth, with more than 18,000 known plant species, including trees more than 2,500 years old. The center makes the Daintree Rainforest accessible to everyone, and I recommend it to anyone.

North Americans don't live in a tropical rainforest, and as interesting as the area is, few plants will survive in our temperate climates. However, lucky designers and gardeners in zone 7 and south can embrace the clinging, climbing fig, *Ficus pumila*. Plants are a mainstay in the Founders Garden in Athens (established in 1936 to honor the members of the first garden club in Amerca, founded in 1891) and smother walls in Charleston and other coastal towns. Plants cling to walls and in early growth look like tentacles slowly eating up

Ficus pumila at
Longwood Gardens

Ficus pumila,
early growth

Ficus pumila
'Variegata'. Photo
by Alan Shapiro.

any rough surface. Soon they will cover walls and make inanimate objects like the famous ficus pillars at Longwood Gardens come alive.

This East Asian species has two phases, a juvenile and adult phase. In the juvenile phase, plants bear thin, small (½- to 1-inch-long), obviously veined dark green leaves. The leaves, with a rounded heart-shaped base and blunt tip, are smooth, and although they appear leathery, they are quite pliable. The slender brown stems root where the nodes touch, much like English ivy and Virginia creeper. The juvenile phase persists for many years, and these small leaves can cover significant areas. In fact, in marginal areas, such as Athens, hard frosts generally knock the plants back, and the mature phase never occurs. Only in frost-free areas and when plants reach at least 5 feet high might they produce leaves up to 4 inches long on a much longer petiole. They may even produce small purple fruit. I have seen plants become awful aggressive weeds in south Texas or southern California, where the lack of frost allows them to cloak large trees and to sneak into places they are not wanted. To be sure, this is not a no-maintenance plant, and if the weather does not control them, plants must be cut back and controlled. If that is too much work, don't plant it.

However, make no mistake about it, most of us in marginal area who are fortunate enough to enjoy these beautiful foliage plants will always be looking at the juvenile growth and not care what it is called. Place in a sheltered area on walls that maintain heat in the evening for fastest growth. And if plants cannot be grown outdoors, you can still bring potted plants inside in baskets, terrariums, and mixed foliage containers.

Occasionally, cultivars like 'Sonny', with white margins, and 'Variegata', with marbled white to cream leaves, may be found.

Propagation
From semi-hardwood cuttings, any time during the season. They may be peeled off the wall, and plants will quickly root at the nodes.

Method of climbing
Plants produce root-bearing stems and will climb any rough surface. Brick walls are easily covered.

Etymology
Ficus, Latin name for the edible fig, *F. carica*; *pumila*, dwarf.

Gelsemium (gell-sem'ee-um)

Carolina jasmine, yellow jessamine

Loganiaceae

Driving down the road past Classic Groundcovers, a well-known nursery in Athens, I always see the dozen or so vines of *Gelsemium sempervirens* covering the green fence. These woody evergreens clamber over and above the fence to fall back upon themselves. They are beautiful in the winter, with their narrow, shiny, ovate to elliptical evergreen foliage reflecting the low-lying sun; and in the spring, the deep green is covered with golden yellow flowers that fill the still air with perfume. Fences are not the only thing they can climb; they can shinny up arbors, tall trees, and of course be the bane of the mailman. Strong pruning is recommended to keep them in bounds. If plants are sited without something to climb on, they will make large mounds, and are quite beautiful shrubs. The 1½-inch-long flowers usually occur singly and resemble bright funnels; they are borne in the leaf axils, which accounts for their number. In Athens, they start to flower in late February or early March and continue for about six weeks.

Gelsemium sempervirens, habit

Gelsemium sempervirens

Plants are native from Virginia to Florida and west to Texas. In the wild, they are extraordinary when in flower but once finished, slide back into obscurity. They grow well in zones 6–9, but may be damaged by hard winters. Otherwise, this is an easy plant to grow, trouble-free and quite wonderful. Full sun is recommended for best flowering, but plants grow well in afternoon shade.

'Pride of Augusta' is a double-flowering selection of *Gelsemium sempervirens*.

Other species

Gelsemium rankinii, swamp jessamine, is also native to the Southeast, although not quite as hardy as *G. sempervirens*. However, plants flower as well in the fall as they do in spring. Unfortunately, the flowers, which occur in two- to three-flowered inflorescences, are not fragrant. Probably cold hardy to zone 7. Not as common as *G. sempervirens* but an equally good performer.

Propagation

From semi-hardwood cuttings in the summer.

Method of climbing

Plants are twiners and will climb up structures and soon enough around themselves.

Etymology

Gelsemium, Latin version of *gelsomino*, the Italian name for jasmine; *sempervirens*, evergreen. Jessamine, the old name for jasmine.

Gurania (gur-an'ee-a)
   jungle cucumber
   Cucurbitaceae

I was talking about this book with Judy Cant, my colleague at the Niagara Parks School of Horticulture and an excellent plantsperson. She is as knowledgeable about tropicals as anyone I know, and she asked, "Did you include jungle cucumber? It is truly beautiful, but few people know of it." She noticed my blank expression and took pity on me. "Come on," she said. We grabbed Loren Hallstrom, a keen student, who was as thrilled to learn a new plant as I was, and off we went across campus to the butterfly conservatory.

As I looked at this thing, I knew it was obviously in the cucumber family; it twisted and climbed up a large structure, holding itself in place with coiled tendrils. The leaves are 3 to 4 inches across, simple to palmate, but so much variability occurs among flowers and foliage that it is difficult to tell the difference between the perhaps fifty species in the genus. Flowers are characterized by the bright orange to red sepals, a character not usually found in the cucumber family. The petals are tiny, yellow, and mostly hidden by the large sepals. The flowers are arranged in many-flowered inflorescences, and although individual flowers persist for only a day or so, the inflorescence may last for weeks. Plants are monoecious, meaning that flowers are either male or female, but both male and female flowers are produced on a single plant. Like many cucumber relatives, they are not both produced on one plant at the same time, so plant-to-plant movement by pollinators is necessary for fertilization. The female flowers will produce green, pickle-sized fruits once pollinated. It made great sense to see *Gurania malacophylla* in the Niagara Parks Butterfly Conservatory with Judy and Loren, as plants are a favorite of king swallowtail butterflies and hummingbirds.

I have never seen plants being offered for sale for home gardeners. So the question comes up—why should it be included in a book for gardeners, the great majority of whom have never heard of it and may not be able to find it? Well, plants are easy to grow from seed, which are occasionally offered and may be fun to try. Who needs a better reason than that?

Gurania malacophylla. Photo by Loren Hallstrom.

Gurania malacophylla with swallowtail butterfly. Photo by Loren Hallstrom.

Propagation
From seeds, just like cucumbers and gourds.

Method of climbing
Plants produce tendrils at the nodes and will cling to anything and help the plant grow upward.

Etymology
Gurania, an anagram of *Anguria*, the old name for the genus. Jungle cucumber, makes sense as to location and fruit.

Hedera (hed′er-a)
ivy
Araliaceae

I hesitate to include ivies in this book because as functional and beautiful as they may be, they are listed as noxious or invasive plants in many states. Yet to dismiss a whole group of plants as being universally bad is to dismiss baseball as being universally boring. All depends on your point of view.

No doubt some places are awash in ivy. States like Oregon and Washington have No Ivy Leagues and other aggressive programs to discourage its production and sale, and there is little doubt that plants can roam. However, in many areas, even where plants overwinter, cold temperatures control the maturation of the vines. Ivies have a juvenile stage, where plants never flower or fruit. This stage is what is purchased in containers, and it is what is used as groundcovers and vines. I have grown English ivy as a groundcover for decades and have yet to see a single flower. I do not allow them to grow up the trees, mainly because I like my tree trunks naked; however, I have seen controlled tree-climbing, which works only if you have garden gnomes pruning the vines to the desired height each year. The mature phase may never occur, but if plants are aggressive in frost-free or mild-winter states, they can produce flowers and fruit after they have scaled tall trees or leapt tall buildings. Although stem pieces may drop to the ground and root, the invasiveness of ivies mainly results from the seeds being dispersed by birds or falling in the woods. That is not to say ivies are not aggressive, or that your life's obsession may be to eradicate the suckers, but I'd like to do that with dandelions as well. And to be sure, the dozens of cultivars with ornamental foliage are generally far slower to grow and far less prone to ever reaching a mature phase than the species themselves. While plants are usually associated with being groundcovers, they are certainly ornamental sheathing a door or greening up a wall.

Hedera helix at
Longwood

I recommend reading a page from Paghat's Garden on the issue of invasiveness of ivies (www.paghat.com/ivy.html), in which the author states similar views but in far more detail. Also for ivy lovers or detractors, the American Ivy Society (www.ivy.org) is worth a visit.

Hedera colchica (kol' chi-ka)
Persian ivy
zones 6b–9

Nearly all the ivy I see as I walk or drive down shaded residential areas is English ivy (*Hedera helix*). For good reason, as it is cold hardy, grows aggressively, and is cheap and easy to find in any plant outlet. However, where I see Persian ivy, a plant native to Turkey and the Caucasus region, I am impressed with the leathery, larger leaves (5 to 6 inches across), each with prominent veins beneath and with a heart-shaped base and pointed leaf tip. Juvenile leaves will be the norm unless the plants get out of hand, at which time, plants will

Hedera colchica 'Sulphur Heart'

produce more rounded leaves and white flowers and black fruit. Keep plants cut back so mature foliage does not occur. By the way, some people find the crushed leaves smell a little like celery. Distinctive. The green juvenile leaves of the species are ornamental; however, a few cultivars are available.

'Dentata' is popular with even larger leaves and dentate (serrations pointing up) margins on heart-shaped leaves. Quite aggressive, get serious with the pruning here.

'Dentata Variegata' is similar in look and habit but with cream-colored margins and grayish mottling on the leaves.

'My Heart' has essentially unlobed dark green 3- to 5-inch-wide foliage, slightly puckered and leathery.

'Sulphur Heart' has light green, almost entire leaves with yellow blotches on the blade.

Hedera helix (hee′lix)
English ivy
zones 4–8

When I first set eyes on the ugly red clay beneath the handsome white oaks in our first home in Athens, this Montreal boy was definitely at a loss. Loved the trees, hated the dirt. When I realized that English ivy, only ever seen as a houseplant in Quebec, would work as a groundcover, I jumped at the opportunity. Heck, everybody had it. So I found some people to dig out patches of their ivy and willingly pass them on to me. I became an instant believer in southern hospitality, and I threw the rooted stems in the ground. They seemed to take forever to grow, so I found more willing gardeners (not hard to do) and put more in. I even asked propagation students, who were using ivy to demonstrate stem rooting, for their plants.

Three years later, they were starting to roam. Five years later they were climbing the trees; eight years later they filled in everywhere. I can moan about how I had to rip the plants from the trees. I can complain about the

Hedera helix at Chanticleer

need to keep the edges of the paths trimmed every year and mutter about keeping it off the azaleas and rhodies. However, that is part of gardening, and for me the net positive aspects of the planting were far greater than the negative. The ground is green, soil erosion is negligible, and they acted as cool barriers for the roots of camellias and rhododendrons when they were first planted. As my back and I get older, the yearly maintenance is more of a chore, but I have no regrets.

Plants are native to northern Europe, into Scandinavia and Russia, so they are more cold hardy than many people realize. And as mentioned in the opening remarks, this plant is not for everyone. Don't use it on Pacific West Coast; it has proven to be a liability there. If it is in your garden, keep it under control. Don't let it climb trees (it does nothing for the tree, and it will flower and seed), and keep it out of places you don't want it to be. That is not easy at times, admittedly. It is far more useful as a groundcover than a vine, and covering ground is what it does. So don't blame the plant if it is successful. If removal is necessary to save your sanity, be patient, hire strong backs if you can, and dig away. Plants are Roundup-sensitive, but don't expect miracles.

English ivies are like daylilies, clematis, and peonies in that there are hundreds of cultivars in different colors, sizes, and leaf shapes. The Pierot system, developed by Susan Pierot in 1974 and adopted by the American Ivy Society as a consistent and convenient way to identify ivy, recognizes eight categories of leaf shapes. Numerous sources list cultivars ranging from the white-edged

Hedera helix 'Buttercup'

'Anne Marie' and the yellow 'Buttercup' to the miniature 'Tussie Mussie' and the white-veined 'Thornhill', and all the stops along the way. Since I have not tried them all, and have no intention to, I further scrutinized the AIS site and noted that since 2001, they have selected an Ivy of the Year. So, if you're not sure what to try, give these interesting selections of *Hedera helix* a go: 'Lady Frances' (2001), 'Teardrop' (2002), 'Golden Ingot' (2003), 'Duck Foot' (2004), 'Misty' (2005), 'Anita' (2006), 'Shamrock' (2007), 'Gold Child' (2008), and 'Eva' (2009).

Other species and cultivars

Hedera algeriensis, Algerian ivy, has larger leaves than English ivy but is winter hardy only to about zone 7. Plants produce three- to seven-lobed glossy green 6-inch leaves. 'Gloire de Marengo' has a blend of light and dark on the leaf blade with a creamy white margin.

Propagation

Ivies are easily propagated from stems. Cut a four- to five-node stem, place horizontally in a tray of soil, pin the stem down at the nodes with bobby pins, and roots will form at each node. Plants can then be cut in rooted segments and placed where desired.

Method of climbing

Plants produce root-bearing stems and will climb any rough surface. Brick walls and rough tree bark are preferred surfaces.

Etymology

Hedera, Latin name for ivy; *algeriensis*, Algerian; *colchica*, from Colchis, an ancient state, mostly ascribed to what is now the western part of Georgia—in Greek mythology, Colchis was the home of Aeëtes and Medea and the destination of the Argonauts; *helix*, Greek for anything of spiral shape, thus applied to twining plants.

Hydrangea (hy-drane'gee-a)
Hydrangeaceae

I have always loved the climbing species in this genus, once known as *Hydrangea petiolaris*, now called *H. anomala* ssp. *petiolaris*, commonly known as climbing hydrangea. I've watched it climb brick chimneys and stone walls from England to Canada, from the Midwest to the Pacific Northwest. The leaves are heart-shaped, and the fertile flowers are much like lacecap hydrangea blooms, but not as attractive. The ornamental value comes from the persistent clusters of as whitish sepals attached to the sides of the fertile flowers.

On mature plants, I also enjoy the strong, manly stems, as thick as the Incredible Hulk's biceps, and all with exfoliating shaggy bark. Plants are native to Japan and China and have been called the best vine in cultivation. Provide this big, strong plant with a strong, rough structure upon which to cling—the operative word here is "strong."

I had a good deal of trouble trying to tell the three climbing hydrangeas apart, but I think I figured the suckers out. See *Decumaria* and *Schizophragma* for more details.

None of the cultivars of *Hydrangea anomala* ssp. *petiolaris* are easily found in the trade, but they are available, with a little digging.

'Firefly' provides the large white flowers typical of a climbing hydrangea but also produces really interesting variegated green and yellow foliage. The foliage is at its best in spring, when leaves are young. As the season progresses, the variegation becomes less intense. Plants were developed by Dan Benarcik, the talented horticulturist at Chanticleer, in Wayne, Pennsylvania.

'Mirranda' is also unusual in that it has heart-shaped green foliage with irregular yellow margins. The leaf margins may fade to creamy white as the

Hydrangea anomala ssp. *petiolaris*, covering wall at Chanticleer

Hydrangea anomala ssp. *petiolaris*

Hydrangea anomala ssp. *petiolaris* 'Firefly'. Photo by Dan Benarcik.

Hydrangea anomala ssp. *petiolaris* 'Firefly', habit. Photo by Dan Benarcik.

Hydrangea anomala ssp. *petiolaris* 'Skylands Giant'. Photo by Tim Wood.

summer progresses. Leaves persist into autumn with little fall color. Launched by Dan Heims of Terra Nova Nurseries, Oregon.

'Skylands Giant' came from Barry Yinger many years ago and is said to be an even more vigorous form of the climber. Quite impressive.

Propagation

Seeds can be directly sown in containers. My colleague Michael Dirr found cold treatment useful for more uniform germination. Dirr also notes the difficulty of rooting terminal cuttings; percentages of 5 percent were not uncommon.

Method of climbing

Like Boston ivy, plants produce clinging holdfasts and use these like cement to help it climb. Rough surfaces like bark, stucco, and brick are penetrated without a second thought.

Etymology

Hydrangea, from the Greek, *hydōr* ("water") and *angos* ("jar"), in reference to the cup-shaped fruits; *anomala*, unusual, deviating from the norm; *petiolaris*, with a particularly long petiole.

Ipomoea (ih-poe-mee′a)
   morning glory
   Convolvulaceae

This is a great genus of wonderful tropical vines. Unfortunately, all are annual and must be replanted every year. But then, so do tomatoes. Morning glory vine (*Ipomoea tricolor*) has been around forever, and in fact so have the weedy cypress vine (*I. quamoclit*) and the somewhat less weedy cardinal flower (*I. coccinea*). They are all loved and cussed to certain degrees by gardeners throughout the country, on the one hand for their beauty, on the other for their reseeding tendencies. However, others in the genus have maintained a bit of star quality about them, in particular, moonflower, *I. alba*, planted to make gardeners feel good about the evening and for all their children who were put to bed with Peter and Jean Loewer's classic book, *The Moonflower*. A great plant, an even better book. And it is only in the last twenty years or so that the lowly sweet potato (*I. batatas*), grown as a staple food for centuries, became the ornamental star it is today.

Ipomoea alba (al′ba)

moonflower

annual

I think my horticultural education in Montreal was somewhat lacking, as I knew nothing of moonflowers or that any plants would bloom at night. Here is a plant that is simply enchanting, beautiful, and wonderfully fragrant to boot. The large clean white flowers open in late afternoon and into the evening, and on a moonlit night are like white flying saucers. The vines are vigorous and can be used to great effect climbing up porches, covering stone walls, or on trellises. Put them where you can also enjoy the fragrance. Collect the weird-looking fruit when they turn gray and keep the seeds for next spring.

Ipomoea alba, habit

Ipomoea alba

Ipomoea alba, fruit.
Photo by Robert Bowden.

Plants are still occasionally found under the old name *Calonyction aculeatum*. Isn't that a good change!

Ipomoea batatas (ba-ta′tas)
sweet potato
annual

Sweet potatoes have been domesticated for at least 5,000 years. They likely originated in Mexico and parts of South America and have been grown as a starch crop for both human and animal food. Recent statistics from the Food and Agriculture Organization show that over 127 million tons of sweet potatoes are produced, much of it from China. In the United States, sweet potatoes are also raised in areas where heat and water can be provided. Louisiana was one of the first states to establish a sweet potato industry, and today many states produce and ship sweet potatoes including North Carolina, Mississippi, and California. The tubers are rich in complex carbohydrates, dietary fiber, and vitamins A, C, and B6. They were an important part of the American diet in the nineteenth and twentieth centuries, particularly in the South; however, as times improved, the use of sweet potatoes declined from a U.S. per capita consumption of 31 lbs in 1920 to less than 4 lbs today.

I wrote this short history of sweet potatoes to illustrate the fact that many food crops can be ornamental but also to illustrate how times have changed. I know a lot more people raising sweet potatoes for the look of the plant rather than for the diet of the gardener.

Sweet potatoes produce twisting stems and will climb if trained and sometimes if not trained! However, most gardeners use them as container plants to run out and over the ground, providing ornamental foliage to contrast with other plants in the garden. Plants have heart-shaped alternate leaves, generally three- to five-lobed or entire. The tuber is formed in the fall, and the longer the plant can stay in the soil, the larger the tuber will be. Ornamental sweet potatoes are quite edible, although the tastiest cultivars have been bred for flavor and are not particularly ornamental. The terms "sweet potato" and "yam" are often used interchangeably in North America, but they are quite different plants. Yams belong to the genus *Dioscorea* and are in an entirely different family (Dioscoreaceae). Other than both having underground edible tubers, there are few other similarities.

Plants are grown in full sun, in reasonably well-drained soils. They require little care except for the occasional watering. They can overwhelm other plants, but cutting back hard does not hurt them at all. Placing plants in containers quells their appetite for acreage somewhat. If space is a problem, selecting some of the newer cultivars (which see) helps keep plants under control. The biggest pain is the sweet potato looper—a caterpillar that chews holes in the leaves. Some years are better than others, and some cultivars are less tasty to the critters than others, but they can be a problem, regardless of cultivar. Remove all dead foliage in the winter and rotate crops in the garden to reduce incidence of this pest. If they are a headache, using a product containing *Bacillus thuringiensis* (Bt) is the most appropriate control. Apply on the undersides of the leaves in the spring. Sweet potato whitefly can be a problem in the greenhouse but is seldom one in the landscape.

The two most important cultivars are 'Blackie' and 'Margarita'; however, their success has led to many more introductions.

'Blackie' supposedly was rescued from the reject pile of sweet potatoes being evaluated for their flavor content in a research station in Monroe, Louisiana. Plants have dark purple, deeply lobed leaves and are very vigorous. It is still as good as it gets for vigorous plants with lobed leaves. The success of 'Blackie' led to the selection and breeding of numerous other dark-leaved forms.

Chillin' series includes 'Chillin' Limeade', a knockoff of 'Margarita', 'Chillin' Blackberry Heart', a knockoff of 'Purple Heart', and 'Chillin' Blackberry Star', a knockoff of 'Blackie'.

Ipomoea batatas 'Margarita'

Ipomoea
batatas
'Blackie'

Ipomoea batatas
'Margarita'

'Margarita' was introduced to commerce in 1994 by the author, who'd received a plant from Hunter Stubbs of North Carolina. The chartreuse leaves were an immediate hit for gardeners and landscapers alike. Both lobed and heart-shaped leaves are produced on the same plant. It is by far the most common ornamental sweet potato cultivar in the world. Other chartreuse forms have been introduced since and are worthy of planting.

'Purple Heart' is similar to 'Blackie', but the leaves are mostly unlobed and heart-shaped. 'Ace of Spades' is similar if not the same. An excellent plant.

Sidekick series was released in 2008 and includes 'Sidekick Lime' and 'Sidekick Black Heart'. The latter performed very well in the Trial Gardens at UGA.

Sweet Caroline series was developed over many years by the excellent breeding of Ken Pecota and his colleagues at North Carolina State University. In 2002, four cultivars were introduced with the Sweet Caroline name. They were 'Sweet Caroline Green', 'Sweet Caroline Light Green', 'Sweet Caroline

Ipomoea batatas 'Sidekick Black Heart'

Bronze', and 'Sweet Caroline Purple'. This was followed by 'Sweet Caroline Bewitched'. All are more compact than the "old" forms; colors vary slightly from the "old" forms. In our trials, 'Bewitched' was excellent. Leaves of plants in this series tend to be deeply lobed.

Sweet Caroline Sweetheart series was the followup. The leaves are mostly heart-shaped, and plants were also selected for compactness and restrained growth (which can certainly be a good thing). Cultivars include 'Sweet Caroline Sweetheart Light Green', 'Sweet Caroline Sweetheart Purple', and 'Sweet Caroline Sweetheart Red'.

'Tricolor' ('Pink Frost') is an old-fashioned, much more restrained cultivar with three-colored slightly lobed leaves. A wonderful but very slow-growing plant.

Ipomoea batatas 'Sweet Caroline Bronze'

Ipomoea batatas
'Sweet Caroline
Sweetheart Red'

Ipomoea batatas
'Sweet Caroline
Bewitched'

Ipomoea batatas
'Tricolor'

Ipomoea lobata (low-bah'ta)

Spanish flag

annual

I believe this is one of the most underused vines today. Plants are easy to raise from seed, they grow rapidly but don't eat the house, and they produce elegant flowers from midsummer to fall. I am not sure why they are not at least as popular as sweet peas or moonflower, but perhaps their day will come.

Plants produce 8- to 15-foot-long stems with 3- to 4-inch-long leaves, generally with three lobes and serrated margins. The leaves are generally disease- and insect-free, but plants are grown for their flowers, not their foliage. Flowers are small but numerous; each thin flower is only 1 to 1½ inches long and ends in a shallow five-lobed apex. The inflorescences, which form in the axils of the leaves, are forked at the first branching point, resulting in up to twenty flowers per inflorescence. They are orange-scarlet as they open, then fade to yellow, then to white. As more clusters form, the potpourri of colors is quite

Ipomoea lobata, habit

Ipomoea lobata

wonderful. The flowers somewhat resemble those of sweet peas, and it turns out this is the only species in the genus with bilaterally symmetrical flowers (having only one plane of symmetry, which can be divided into two equal halves). This is likely a totally useless piece of information but may explain why the plants were in a different genus (*Mina*) for so many years.

I often give seeds of Spanish flag to my students to grow. Few of them know anything about growing plants. That they are successful demonstrates the ease of growing, that they are ecstatic shows they have good taste.

Ipomoea tricolor (tri′col-or)
morning glory
annual

Because of good taste, I can't tell you how I have cussed and cursed morning glories in the garden. When I see morning glories blooming in other gardens, I revel in their beauty. The heart-shaped leaves cover the 15-foot vines and the 2- to 4-inch-wide funnel-shaped flowers are spectacular. The invasive species has blue flowers with a white tube and some yellow in the center. However, how these plants can reseed! I know I am not the only gardener who is digging out seedlings every spring, sometimes from plants that were in the garden three years ago. I love the morning glories, but I could do without the additional weeding.

Morning glory is a common name for a number of closely related species, including *Ipomoea purpurea*, *I. hederacea*, and *I. nil*. All have similar flowers. Some are much hairier than others (*I. purpurea*); some have three-lobed leaves (*I. hederacea*, *I. nil*). *Ipomoea purpurea*, *I. hederacea*, and *I. nil* have a three-lobed stigma; *I. tricolor* is two-lobed. But without a serious examination, you would be hard-pressed to know the parentage of the vine you are planting.

We soak the seeds for about four hours before we plant them, either indoors three to four weeks before the expected last frost if we want a quicker start, or outdoors after all threat of frost is past.

Many cultivars have been introduced from the various species. Some have been around for many years; most come and go quickly. Cultivars may be listed under numerous species, but essentially they are grown in the same way and provide large colorful flowers, often with quite handsome foliage.

'Black Knight' has deep purple flowers with a rose and white throat.

'Candy Pink' has 3- to 4-inch-wide pink flowers with a white center. From the center, five lighter pink lines travel to the edge of the flower.

Ipomoea tricolor, eating garden. Photo by Suzy Bales.

'Crimson Rambler' produces crimson flowers with white centers.

'Flying Saucers' has flowers with strips of white and blue throughout. Unique.

Good Morning series caught a lot of eyes when we had them in the Trial Gardens at UGA. Flowers may be blue, pink, red, or violet, but the foliage is variegated green and white. Plants do not climb as vigorously as other cultivars here, which may not be a bad thing.

'Grandpa Ott' bears large violet-blue flowers with reddish center.

'Heavenly Blue' is the best known of all the morning glories. Large sky blue flowers with white to yellowish throats adorn this vine.

'Minibar Rose' has interesting small green and white foliage and small rosy red flowers. Highly recommended for planters or baskets.

Mt. Fuji mix consists of plants with blue and white, red and white, and pink and white flowers. 'Mt. Fuji Blue' seems to be the most available.

'Pearly Gates' produces wonderful satiny white flowers with yellow throats.

'Scarlett O'Hara' has large wine-red flowers on a vigorous climber.

'Split Personality' has magenta-cherry flowers that are shallowly split and large white centers.

'Sunrise Serenade' has unusual double flowers. They are large, ruby-red in color, and definitely catch the eye.

Sun Smile series provides bushy plants that are much less vigorous climbers. Plants are available in blue, pink, red, and violet.

Ipomoea tricolor

Ipomoea tricolor
'Good Morning Blue'

Ipomoea tricolor
'Heavenly Blue'

Ipomoea tricolor
'Pearly Gates'

Ipomoea tricolor
'Sunrise Serenade'.
Photo by Meg Green.

Tie Dye series has flowers with a mishmash of blue and white or pink and white. The patterns resemble a tie-dyed T. Rather gruesome, actually.

Other species and cultivars

Ipomoea coccinea, cardinal flower, is native from Pennsylvania to Georgia, and although the small cardinal red flowers are quite showy, the plants can be quite weedy, hanging on and over anything in their path. The ovate leaves are entire or occasionally coarsely toothed. If sufficient plants are placed in a container or small area and trained together, they can make an impressive show. A wonderful hummingbird attractor.

Ipomoea quamoclit, cypress vine, has leaves that are deeply cut and almost fernlike in appearance. The small scarlet flowers are handsome, and if trained well the plant can provide an impressive show. Similar to cardinal flower, they are hummingbird magnets. They often reseed and out of place can look like climbing weeds. 'Alba' is a white-flowering form.

Ipomoea ×sloteri, cardinal climber, is a hybrid between *I. coccinea* and *I. quamoclit*. Even if it doesn't flower profusely, it is a handsome plant. Its large wonderfully lobed leaves are the best part. When the scarlet flowers do appear, they are butterfly magnets. Plants don't reseed. Much better than either parent.

Ipomoea quamoclit

Ipomoea ×sloteri

Propagation

Most species are propagated from seeds. In general, soaking the seed for four to eight hours helps with germination. Plant seeds and keep moist and warm (70–72F). Sweet potato is easily propagated from terminal cuttings.

Method of climbing

Plants are twiners and twine around structures or other plants. Sweet potato will not climb unless trained to do so.

Etymology

Ipomoea, from the Greek, *ips* ("worm") and *hŏmoious* ("similar to"); *alba*, white; *batatas*, vernacular Haitian Indian name for sweet potato; *coccinea*, scarlet; *lobata*, lobed, referring to the leaves; *quamoclit*, possibly from the Greek, *kuamos* ("bean"); *tricolor*, three colors. Cardinal refers to the color of the flowers; cypress vine, the leaves may remind one of those of a cypress; moonflower, flowers are nocturnal, opening at night; morning glory, flowers open in the morning, close later in the day; Spanish flag, the colors of the flowers are similar to those of the flag of Spain; sweet potato, from the sweet underground tuber.

Jasminum (jaz-mi′num)
   jasmine
   Oleaceae

Some of the hardy jasmines such as *Jasminum nudiflorum* are quite wonderful, showing off bright yellow flowers even before the forsythias. Unfortunately, the climbers in this genus do not possess sufficient cold hardiness to be a mainstay in most temperate gardens, although one or two grow well to zone 7b or 8. The vines are all native to China and are woody plants, generally bearing white or pink tubular flowers in late spring and early summer. Although they may flower the first year they are planted, most are poor annuals, as they will not attain sufficient height nor produce enough flowers to do well outdoors if they are killed by winter.

Today, with the Internet, the choice of climbers that can be obtained is wider, but that does not mean plants are any hardier. If I had a conservatory, I would buy plants of the wonderfully fragrant white-flowered *Jasminum polyanthum*. A great plant, but it will not survive any frost, so I would have to bring them in in the winter. Or I would find some plants of the common jasmine vine, *J. officinale, the* white-flowered jasmine of literature. With its slightly greater hardiness, fragrant flowers, and handsome pinnate leaves, I might spend my money. If I lived in Santa Barbara, I could see the red flower buds give rise to the fragrant, clean white flowers. Hell, I'd make an entire hedge out of it if I could. Exquisite. Without doubt, I'd spend my coins on Fiona Sunrise (= 'Frojas'), a slower growing but eye-catching cultivar with golden foliage.

However, if I could buy but one jasmine, it would be *Jasminum ×stephanense*, a vigorous climber cold hardy to zone 7a or 7b. Plants were bred in Saint-Etienne, France, before 1920 and sold by the Lemoine Nursery of Nancy. The hybrid vigor is the result of a cross between *J. beesianum* and *J. officinale*, and where plants grow to maturity,

Jasminum officinale

Jasminum officinale, habit

Jasminum officinale Fiona Sunrise (= 'Frojas'). Photo by Robert Bowden.

they reach heights of 10 to 15 feet. Both simple and compound leaves on the same plant reflect both parents, and hundreds of wonderfully fragrant pale pink flowers are borne in the spring into the summer. Hardiness is still an issue. Find a sunny, protected location, mulch the plants heavily, and be prepared for significant dieback.

Propagation

Plants of the species can be raised from seed, although uniformity of germination is poor. All can be propagated by terminal cuttings. Use one- or two-node cuttings in spring and early summer and place in warm, moist conditions.

Method of climbing

The long stems will twine around structures or other plants.

Etymology

Jasminum, late medieval Latin version of the Persian name *yāsamīn*; *officinale*, having real or supposed medicinal properties; *polyanthum*, with many flowers; *stephanense*, refers to the town where the hybrid was raised (Stephan is the English version of the French name Etienne).

Jasminum ×stephanense

Lablab (lab′lab)

Fabaceae

Some annual vines are so easy to grow and provide so much enjoyment, they ought to be everywhere. This genus contains one of those no-brainers that is not only fun but has a great name as well. Hyacinth bean (*Lablab purpureus*) was once known as *Dolichos lablab*, but that did not flow off the tongue nearly as well as the new name. As a useless piece of information, you might be interested to know that in South Asia, China, Japan, West Africa, and the Caribbean, non-vining forms of lablab (mainly 'Rongai') are used as cover crops to replace nitrogen and often incorporated with economically important crops like corn and soybeans in a crop rotation plan.

As an ornamental vine, hyacinth bean produces 3- to 4-inch-wide dark green, heavily veined trifoliate leaves and will grow 15 feet in a season. The fragrant lavender flowers, shaped just like those you see on edible beans, are clustered in groups of five and are produced by midsummer. They are colorful and handsome, but it is the dark thin purple beans, each one 4 inches long, that really provide this plant's character. The seeds will also be purple when mature. Some people enjoy eating the beans, and if grown for culinary

Lablab purpureus

Lablab
purpureus,
fruit

purposes, choose cultivars that are day neutral or long day for flowering. Beans are edible only after boiling; they should not be eaten raw.

Plants in the bean family are nitrogen fixers, meaning they produce their own nitrogen, thus high rates of fertility are a waste of money. Plants can be grown up a trellis or a wall and will provide shade on the roof. One of the prettiest sights is a "hedge" of these vines covering a fence in the front of a house. Traffic stopper.

'Albiflorus' is a white-flowered form of *Lablab purpureus* with green fruit.

'Ruby Moon' has darker foliage and fruit.

Propagation
Plants are easily raised from seeds, just like common garden beans. Sow indoors two or three weeks before the expected last frost, or sow in place once soils have warmed up. Seeds can be collected in the fall and stored in a cool, dry place for sowing the next spring.

Method of climbing
Plants are twiners; the stems twine around structures or other plants.

Etymology
Lablab, probably from *labiatus* ("lipped"), in reference to the flowers; *purpureus*, purple. Hyacinth bean, perhaps so named because the color of the bean was reminiscent of the common purple color of hyacinths.

Lathyrus (la'ther-us)
pea
Fabaceae

The genus includes over 100 species, including everlasting pea, *Lathyrus latifolius*, whose rosy purple flowers can be seen naturalized in the southeast coast, and *L. vernus*, spring vetch, with purple flowers. However, the main claim to fame for horticulturists is the sweet pea (*L. odoratus*), an economically important cut flower for over a century. The flowers are cut in greenhouses in Europe, America, and Asia, shipped around the world, and finally find their place in a vase, perfuming homes hundreds of miles away.

While they are wonderful to purchase, they are even more fun to grow. Plants produce winged stems with compound light green foliage and beautiful pea-like flowers in many colors. As a garden plant, they have few demands, but those requirements must be met for successful growing. The most important is to recognize that plants need cool weather to perform well. Therefore, if you live anywhere south of the 40th parallel and not in the mountains, sweet peas should be considered an early spring crop. Below the 30th parallel, they may even be considered a winter crop. When temperatures are consistently above 70F, they grow well but flower poorly. Plants will tolerate the occasional freeze, to about 28F, but cool night temperatures of 48–55F are best for flower production. The other necessity is support to keep them upright. Since plants will be removed by midsummer, something temporary is often used. Many people use a teepee structure fashioned from rough bamboo stems or a similarly inexpensive structure. Recently, dwarf forms have been developed with bushy habits, rendering support superfluous.

The flowers are held on short stems but may be cut and enjoyed in a shallow vase. The fragrance in the garden is fleeting but will be much more obvious when the flowers are brought inside to a warmer environment. If not cut, dark drooping pea fruit will occur. Seeds can be collected for next year.

Dozens and dozens of cultivars of *Lathyrus odoratus* have been bred over the years, mainly as a response to the cut flower trade. There are cultivars with wavy, frilly, or semi-double blooms, and flowers with two colors (bicolors), flecks, picotees, or ruffles. Unfortunately, the incredible diversity of the old-fashioned and multicolored tall vining forms is not easily available to the

Lathyrus odoratus, blue

Lathyrus odoratus, red

Lathyrus odoratus, fruit

Lathyrus odoratus, bicolor

gardener, but the dwarf forms, including Knee High series, about 3 feet tall, are relatively easy to find. Good seed sources will have a half-dozen choices of sweet peas.

Propagation

Plants are easily raised from seeds. In frost or in minimal frost climates, seeds may be sown in late fall or in a cold frame and placed outdoors in February. In temperate climates, sow seeds indoors or in a cold frame and transplant as soon as possible but once hard frosts are no longer expected.

Method of climbing

Plants have tendrils, like all climbing peas, and are self-supporting.

Etymology

Lathyrus, from the Greek, *lathyros* ("pea"); *latifolius*, broad-leaved; *odoratus*, fragrant; *vernus*, spring. Sweet pea, from the fragrance of the flowers.

Lonicera (lon-iss'er-a)
honeysuckle
Caprifoliaceae

This is a large genus of plants, consisting of over 180 species of woody ornamental shrubs and climbers. Honeysuckles are generally easy to grow and quite cold hardy, and the flowers, although small, are pleasing to the eye and often quite fragrant. Ornamental red, black, or blue fruit is not uncommon in many of the bush species but far less common on the climbers.

Numerous vines have been identified in the genus, and natural and man-made hybrids are quite common, particularly in European gardens. In North America, only three or four species are easily available, although a good number of hybrids and cultivars may be found.

Lonicera ×heckrottii (hek-rot′ee-eye)
goldflame honeysuckle
zones 5–9

I really enjoy this vine because it is easy to grow, has handsome and slightly fragrant flowers, and does not take over the world as other honeysuckles are apt to do. The plant is relatively easy to identify from the opposite leaves at the bottom of the plant, the fused bases (connate) of the leaves at the top of the plant, and the deep red flower buds that open to yellow. The connate leaves are particularly eye-catching as they form a bowl for the developing flowers. Blossoms will continue to be produced as long as new growth occurs, but flowering is at its peak in late spring and summer with sporadic flowering in the fall. The scent is pleasant but will not knock you over, and spring flowers tend to be more fragrant than later ones. I have seen no fruit, nor have I seen this plant to be a problem getting out of hand.

Plants will climb, if supported, or ramble over fences and shrubs, with stems 10 to 15 feet long if unchecked. As with most woody vines, the base of the plant becomes naked over time. If bare legs are a problem, place it behind other plants in the garden. Aphids can be a nuisance. If plants get too tall, they may be cut back after flowering.

The origin of the hybrid is not exactly known, but most experts suggest it is a cross between trumpet honeysuckle, *Lonicera sempervirens*, and *L. ×americana*.

'Goldflame' is similar to *Lonicera ×heckrottii* but is described as having darker red flower buds and deeper green leaves.

Lonicera japonica (ja-pon′i-ka)
Japanese honeysuckle
zones 4–9

I think of this plant as I think of purple loosestrife, *Lythrum salicaria*. Both are quite beautiful, both have lots of reasons to incorporate them in the garden—and both are obnoxiously invasive. *Lonicera japonica* was introduced from Asia in the mid 1800s for erosion control, and like kudzu, has outdone itself.

Plants are more scramblers than vines and make excellent hillside plants for sun or partial shade. However, they also scramble over anything that is stationary and end up smothering and suffocating other plants. This may not be a problem in a tended garden, but it certainly is when plants escape to the wild. They multiply by seed but mainly through rhizomes and creeping stems.

The opposite leaves are evergreen in the South and mid-Atlantic states but deciduous further north. The paired white flowers turn yellow and are absolutely deliciously fragrant, the main reason unsuspecting gardeners buy the plant. The main cultivar is 'Halliana', otherwise known as Hall's honeysuckle, wonderfully perfumed and incredibly thug-like. Most of the plants for sale are this cultivar. If honeysuckle is a must for your garden, save your back and the woodlands, and purchase goldflame or trumpet honeysuckle.

'Aureoreticulata' bears green leaves with yellow netting. Interesting, to be sure.

'Halliana' has been mentioned. There are too many reasons to stay away from this plant; do not buy or accept from a kind neighbor.

'Purpurea' (var. *purpurea*) has darker, almost purple foliage and flowers purple-red on the outside and white inside. Not as aggressive but use with caution.

Lonicera sempervirens (sem-per-veer′enz)
trumpet honeysuckle
zones 4–9

There are a number of native honeysuckles, but this is one of the best. Plants are native to the eastern and southeastern United States, although they may occur west to Texas. They do not invade, and numerous cultivars are available to help with plant selection. The ovate leaves are opposite and simple, and the two uppermost pairs are connate (see *Lonicera ×heckrottii*). The leaves are deciduous in most climates, but this is one of the earliest to green up in early spring. The flowers occur in three or four whorled inflorescences and are long (1½ to 2 inches) and trumpet-shaped and are obviously four-lobed, unusual with most honeysuckles. The flower color is variable but typically (in the species) is orange-scarlet to red on the outside and yellow to yellow-orange inside. Most flowers occur on old wood, although a few flowers will form on new growth. I believe some of the most handsome honeysuckle flowers occur with this native species and cultivars—the downside is that they are not fragrant.

Plants do best in full sun and are easily propagated from cuttings or seed. If you are in the market for a vining honeysuckle, this is an excellent choice.

'Alabama Crimson' has deep red trumpet flowers.

'Blanche Sandman' also has scarlet flowers with soft yellow centers.

'Cedar Lane' originated from Cedar Lane Farms in Madison, Georgia, and bears scarlet-red flowers. Plants rebloom on new wood.

'John Clayton' produces clear yellow flowers on and off throughout the season. An excellent performer in the Trial Gardens at UGA.

'Magnifica' is one of the many red-flowered forms available (all look about the same). Flowers have yellow centers.

'Sulphurea' is also yellow, a much older introduction, but it is a great grower and can

Lonicera
sempervirens

Lonicera
sempervirens, habit

Lonicera sempervirens
'John Clayton'

be completely covered with sulphur yellow flowers by midsummer. Still one of the better selections of this species.

Other species and cultivars

Lonicera periclymenum, woodbine honeysuckle, is native to Europe and parts of Asia. Plants bear opposite leaves, with no connate bases, and fragrant, tubular, two-lipped creamy white flowers with a purple tinge. In the late summer and fall, red berries often appear. Plants climb 10 to 15 feet; hardy to about zone 4. 'Berries Jubilee' has purple flowers and bright red fruit. 'Harlequin' is best known for its leaves with white margins and pink (outside) and white (inside) flowers.

Lonicera sempervirens
'John Clayton', habit

'Serotina Florida' has dark red flowers on the outside, creamy on the inside. 'Sweet Sue' has creamy white and yellow flowers. 'Winchester' has fragrant flowers that are red, pink, and creamy white at the same time.

Lonicera etrusca, Mediterranean honeysuckle, is best known for the selection 'Superba'. Low care, easy to grow, and bears handsome cream and yellow flowers.

Propagation

Plants are easily raised from seeds. In frost or in minimal frost climates, seeds may be sown in late fall or in a cold frame and placed outdoors in February. In temperate climates, sow seeds indoors or in a cold frame and transplant as soon as possible but once hard frosts are no longer expected.

Method of climbing

Plants are self-supporting with a little help to get them started. The long stems are twiners and will whorl around any structure or even other plants.

Etymology

Lonicera, honors German naturalist and herbalist Adam Lonicer (1528–1586); *japonica*, from Japan; *sempervirens*, evergreen; *periclymenum*, from the Greek, *pĕriklymĕnon* ("honeysuckle"). Honeysuckle, from the fragrance of the flowers.

Lonicera etrusca
'Superba'

Lonicera etrusca
'Superba', habit

Macfadyena (mak-fa-dee′na)
Bignoniaceae

When writing a book about ornamental vines, I constantly debate the merits of including this one or that one. I try not to recommend those without much ornamental value and try to identify the ones that are known to be invasive. I suppose I could include kudzu (*Pueraria montana* var. *lobata*), since it is not a threat in the North (although it has been found as far north as Illinois); however, there are far better annual screening vines for the North, and since kudzu is killed in the winter, no flowers will occur, so why bother? And if you are a gardener and have seen thousands of acres of kudzu eating the South, you know better anyhow.

Such is the problem with cat's claw (*Macfadyena unguis-cati*), except it is really ornamental. If you see this plant shimmering with large yellow flowers, you may feel that you must have one in your garden, but be warned: if you garden in a frost-free area, stay away—it is a kudzu in disguise. I have seen beautiful plants in eastern Australia, where few complaints occurred; however, as spectacular as it is in flower, reports from many parts of North America are overwhelmingly negative. Here are but a few examples—the first from Louisiana, the second from Florida, the third from Arizona—from Dave's Garden (davesgarden.com). You can feel their pain.

> Can anybody provide me with some napalm? Seriously, this is not a friendly vine. It is all over every blighted home in New Orleans, not even Katrina could kill it!

> It smothered 60-year-old camellias, azaleas, trees . . . . The sharp, catlike claws allow it to grip and totally cover anything! Cut it down prior to blooming, or a million more seeds will spread from the long pods.

> This plant is *very invasive*. I have seen it actually lift the shingles off of roofs. It also attaches itself with the "claw" to stucco homes and walls, and when you try to remove it, the stucco comes off with it! . . . *Don't plant this!!!!*

A few nurseries and seed companies sell the plant, and unsuspecting friends may give you a start because it grows so well. It is like the seductive Sirens heard by Odysseus—cover your ears, and eyes, and walk past. Plants are useless in frost areas as they don't flower on new wood, so unless they are used as conservatory plants, they have no future in Michigan. The other good thing is that the name is so unpronounceable, no one will ask for it anyway. Plants may still be listed under the genus *Doxantha*, but "a rose is still a rose."

Propagation

Plants multiply by tubers and seeds. After reading the earlier comments, propagation may not seem too bright an idea. However, for people who wish to keep them in glass-houses and conservatories, they propagate quite easily.

Method of climbing

The tendrils ("cat's claws") at the nodes allow them to secure a hold on almost anything.

Etymology

Macfadyena, named for Scottish botanist James Macfadyen (1798–1850); *unguis-cati*, from *unguis* ("furnished with a claw") and *cati* ("cat").

*Macfadyena
unguis-cati*

*Macfadyena
unguis-cati*, habit

Mandevilla (man-de-vil′a)
Apocynaceae

In general, flowers in this genus vary from deep rose to pink, although white flowers may be found with serious hunting. The opposite leaves are quite showy, generally shiny green on the upper sides, dull green beneath, and often pointed at the tip. The flowers are held in few-flowered racemes and open like big periwinkles—a lot bigger, a lot showier, but nevertheless quite closely related (in fact, they are in the same family).

Plants do well outdoors, even in temperate climates. Although warm weather is to their liking, they tolerate cool nights in the 50s and will not decline badly until nights are in the 40s. Full sun is recommended. Copious water and fertilizer will help to establish the vines in the spring as temperatures warm up; however, plants do not need much water once established.

If you are going to bring them in, expect lots of tendrils, which will eat you and your reading lamp. These can be cut back without damaging the plant, so be ruthless. Unfortunately, mandevillas are also quite susceptible to aphids and spider mites, a much bigger problem indoors than out. Makes you think twice about bringing them in. However, you will be pleased once you put them out again and watch them take off.

Mandevilla boliviensis (bow-liv-ee-en′sis)
Bolivian dipladenia
annual

Native to both Bolivia and Ecuador, this species will grow to about 12 feet tall. Plants are well known for their lustrous green 4-inch-long leaves and clusters of three to seven, 2-inch white flowers with orange-yellow centers. A somewhat similar species is *Mandevilla laxa*, Chilean jasmine (although it is native to Argentina, Bolivia, and Peru); the bonus to this plant is the small clusters of fragrant white flowers, each about 2 inches long and narrowly funnel-shaped. Plants grow to about 10 feet in height. Both thrive in full sun and warm temperatures.

Other species and cultivars
Most plants sold today with red and rose flowers are hybrids of some sort, usually combining *Mandevilla sanderi*, *M. splendens*, and *M. ×amabilis* or other combinations of the 100 or so species in the genus. *Mandevilla sanderi* has leathery leaves and large flowers, up to 3 inches wide. Flowers are generally rose-pink with a yellow eye. *Mandevilla splendens* sports leaves nearly 8

inches long and the largest flowers in the culti-vated species, up to 5 inches wide. Flowers are usually rose-colored.

Dozens of cultivars have been selected and bred. However, garden centers in temperate climates seldom stock more than a couple, and even in the Deep South, choices are limited. The best way to find more than one or two choices is to check online.

'Alice du Pont' is the most common culti-var in commerce. She bears light pink, some-times described as icy pink, flowers with a deep red throat. Likely a selection of *Mande-villa ×amabilis*. Plants grow 10 to 12 feet.

'Bride's Cascade' provides white flowers with yellow centers, and lustrous shiny green leaves.

'Cotton Candy' has soft pink flowers and shiny green leaves. Very handsome.

'Moonlight Parfait' has interesting white flowers that fade to blush, particularly in tem-perate climates. The rose-like pink-red center is quite obvious.

'Pink Parfait' is quite interesting in that plants bear double flowers, somewhat like a rose. Certainly not my favorite; if I want a rose, I'll buy a rose.

'Red Fury' has bright red trumpet-like flow-ers with a yellow throat.

'Red Riding Hood' is an old-fashioned almost dwarf form, with stems only 4 to 6 feet long. Plants bear deep rosy pink flowers with yellow centers.

Rio series is one of the best for containers in that the plants do not climb, at least outdoors. We trialed a 'Rio Deep Red' and 'Rio Pink', and both retained heights of less than 2 feet and produced handsome flowers late summer and fall. Plants may start to climb after a year or so.

Mandevilla ×amabilis 'Alice du Pont'. Photo by Alan Shapiro.

Mandevilla 'Rio Deep Red'

Mandevilla 'Sun Parasol Red'

Mandevilla 'Sun Parasol Stars and Stripes'

Sun Parasol series has been available since 2003 and brings a remarkable range of colors to the American gardener. The original introductions of *Mandevilla sanderi* were crimson, pink, dark red, and cream-pink. Even larger plants and flowers can be found on 'Giant White', 'Giant Pink', and 'Giant Crimson', all hybrids. 'Pretty Crimson' and 'Pretty White' are smaller and may be more appropriate for smaller gardens. The 2009 introductions are 'Lush Crimson', 'Burgundy', and the wonderful 'Stars and Stripes' with red and white flowers.

'Tango Twirl' has light pink, fully double flowers. New, unique, and show-stopping.

Velvet series was developed by Lake Area Nursery in Hawthorne, Florida, and includes cultivars in red, pink, white, and scarlet. All produce large (3- to 4-inch-wide) flowers and are vigorous growers. A smaller-flowered form, 'Red Velvet Petite', has also been developed.

Propagation
Plants can be easily grown from cuttings, but most cultivars are patented (you will see a PP number on the tag), so propagation is not allowed. However, that rule applies to commercial production, so if you are not selling plants, do not worry about it.

Method of climbing
By twining stems; they need some help when tendrils first start climbing.

Etymology
Mandevilla, named for Henry John Mandeville (1773–1861), British minister in Buenos Aires; *amabilis*, showy; *boliviensis*, from Bolivia; *laxa*, loose; *sanderi*, for German-born British nurseryman Henry Frederick Conrad Sander (1847–1920); *splendens*, splendid. Dipladenia was the old botanical genus name for mandevilla.

Manettia (ma-net′ee-a)
firecracker plant
Rubiaceae

These plants are generally evergreen climbers with dark green opposite leaves and small cylindrical flowers. Over eighty species have been cataloged; the two that gardeners are most likely to find are *Manettia luteorubra* and *M. cordifolia*, both also known as firecracker plants. A number of subtle differences in leaf shape occur; the flowers of the former are a vibrant scarlet-red for more than three-quarters of the length, and bright yellow at the tips, whereas the latter are less obviously bicolored. Generally flowers are formed in the axils of the leaves, usually one at a time, occasionally in groups of two. Once plants start to flower, they will continue all season until frost.

Plants grow with twining four-sided stems. The stems are not as obviously squared as those of the mint family, but the characteristic can be observed quite easily. Plants tolerate heat but also do well in cooler summers as annuals. From Montreal, Wisconsin, New York, and south to Texas, gardeners gush over these long-flowering plants. They are listed as growing to 10 feet in height, but 4 feet is more common in temperate zones. Personally, I have trialed these plants a few times and admit to frustration. They tend to struggle and never really want to climb, extending to perhaps 2 feet in height. It may be the heat and humidity in our Athens summer. They are still handsome plants but have been frustrating when we were trying to cover a trellis.

Plants can be brought inside to overwinter in bright light and moderate moisture. They are quite susceptible to whiteflies.

'John Elsley' appears to be a hybrid. It is far more vigorous than either of the species and is the plant of choice. Flowers are scarlet, and I have seen a 6-foot plant almost covered with flowers. Named for one of America's great horticulturists.

Propagation
Plants can be easily grown from terminal cuttings in spring or early summer.

Manettia luteorubra

Manettia 'John Elsley'.
Photo by Alan Shapiro.

Method of climbing

If they decide to climb for you, they would do so with twining stems. Help them out a little to get started.

Etymology

Manettia, named for Saverio Manetti (1723–1785), the prefect of the Florence Botanical Garden; *cordifolia*, heart-shaped leaves; *luteorubra*, for the yellow and red flowers. Firecracker, in reference to the wild, explosive flower colors.

Mascagnia (mas-ka′nee-a)
butterfly vine
Malpighiaceae

I am not sure where we first obtained seeds for these vines, but we knew absolutely nothing about them. I looked it up in leading national and international reference books—nothing. I went online looking for cultural information and finally found a couple of vendors, but they were out of seed. I suppose it is not surprising that few vendors have it since few gardeners outside Texas and perhaps Florida have ever heard of it. That is a shame, for its wonderful flowers, contained growth, and unique fruit are well worth the time and space in the garden. That it belongs to a family that contains nothing you have ever heard of is another hint that it may be difficult to locate. Be a gardener—go hunting.

The most common species is *Mascagnia macroptera*, yellow butterfly vine, a plant that produces dull green leathery leaves on woody stems. The yellow flowers consist of five broad wing-like non-overlapping petals, each petal with fine ciliate hairs on the margins. Plants will grow 10 to 15 feet in warm climates, only about 8 to 10 feet in more temperate zones. It is a woody vine and will not flower and fruit until late summer or the fall if it does not overwinter (zone 8 or 9). In Athens, zone 7b, it is a long wait but well worth it. I doubt that gardeners in Portland, Maine, would have the same patience. In the North, there may not be enough time before frost hits it, but if started a month or so indoors, perhaps so. In fact, while the flowers are quite beautiful, it is the butterfly-like fruits that are really interesting.

The fruits are samaras, like those of maples, and the two broad wings are big enough to remind one of a butterfly. They start green and if sufficient time is available, they turn a bronze-amber. If picked while green, they stay green and are quite useful in dried arrangements.

The other species that I am liking more and more is the lilac butterfly vine, *Mascagnia lilacina*. Equally beautiful, it also appears to have a good bit more

Mascagnia macroptera

Mascagnia macroptera, habit.
Photo by Susan Watkins.

Mascagnia macroptera, fruit

Mascagnia lilacina.
Photo by Alan Shapiro.

cold tolerance, coming back at least in Athens. It has similar foliage, may be more vigorous, and bears lovely lilac to lavender flowers, similar in shape to those of yellow butterfly vine. The fruits are also similar, although not as big.

Although the vines are native to tropical regions, they are quite drought tolerant. Plant in full sun; water as needed.

Propagation

Plants are best increased by stem layering. Lay a long stem on a bed of moist peat moss, secure it at the nodes, and cover the nodes lightly with a thin layer of additional peat. Keep moist, not wet; roots will occur at the nodes. Think of it as English ivy. Seeds and cuttings are also useful, simply less consistent.

Method of climbing

Plants grow by twining stems. They need support to get started, then will climb over themselves.

Etymology

Mascagnia, in honor of famed Italian anatomist Paolo Mascagni (1755–1815); *lilacina*, lilac color; *macroptera*, from *macro* ("large") and *pter* ("wings"), referring to the winged fruit.

Momordica (mo-mor′di-ka)
balsam pear, bitter cucumber
Cucurbitaceae

This is a most interesting genus of ornamental vines for someone wanting a plant combining large flowers, funky fruit, and quite beautiful seeds. Of the forty-five species described, the most common is *Momordica charantia*. We grew this plant for a couple of years and were enthralled with its changes as it grew along our fence. We enjoyed the light green leaves that are almost maple-like, each with five to seven sharp-toothed notched lobes. The monoecious (either male or female) cucumber-like yellow flowers are about 1 inch across with scales or bumps at the base.

A climbing cucumber is all well and good, but the fruits provide the most fun. Think of a 6- to 7-inch-long warty cucumber with lengthwise furrows, and you get the idea. They are hollow in cross-section, with a relatively thin layer of flesh surrounding a central seed cavity filled with large flat seeds. The seeds are white in unripe fruits and ripen to deep red. The fruit is quite edible, and the skin is crunchy when eaten green. Although it can also be eaten when it has started to ripen and turn yellowish, it becomes more bitter as it ripens. The interior of the fruit is sweet when the fruit is ripe, but the skin is quite

Momordica charantia

Momordica charantia, immature fruit. Photo by Meg Green.

Momordica charantia, mature fruit. Photo by Meg Green.

bitter at the time. We seldom had many fruit falling to the ground as many of our Asian visitors asked if they could harvest them.

I rather doubt that my inadequate description makes you want to go out and plant these in your veggie garden, and if you don't crave these in your salad, plants still provide great ornamental value. The best fun occurs as the fruit ripens; each one splits into three divisions and reveals the bright scarlet seeds attached to the interior of the fruit. Like a bad dream from the '60s. The seeds often have a grooved or irregular margin, as if something has taken a small bite out of them. At this time, late summer and fall, the plant will bear yellow flowers, green fruit, and red seeds at the same time.

Other species may be purchased; all are similar but not as ornamental as *Momordica charantia*. Plants do well in temperate climates but are not frost tolerant.

Propagation
Plants are easily propagated by seed, similar to a cucumber.

Method of climbing
Plants produce curly tendrils at the leaf nodes. They are self-supporting if provided with wires or other narrow structures to curl around.

Etymology
Momordica, from the Latin, *mordeo* ("to bite"), perhaps because the margins of the seeds are somewhat misshapen and appear to have been chewed; *charantia*, unknown, appears to be a pre-Linnaean name.

Momordica charantia, fruit beginning to split.
Photo by Meg Green.

Momordica charantia, seeds and interior of fruit. Photo by Meg Green.

Oxypetalum (ox-ee-pet′a-lum)
tweedia
Asclepiadaceae

With a name like tweedia, it is almost impossible not to love this relative of butterfly weed and *Hoya*. Add to that the velvety leaves and some of the finest blue flowers in the plant kingdom (described as glacier blue to bright sky blue to clear pale blue), and it becomes a must-try plant. Having grown tweedia, *Oxypetalum caeruleum* (syn. *Tweedia caerulea*), on many occasions, I have no doubt that, when the flowers open, you will fall in love with them. I conducted a good deal of research on this plant, as I believed it to have excellent potential as a cut flower. In fact, it has become relatively common in high-end florist shops. The data showed that under controlled experimental conditions, plants are good climbers with long-day conditions, bright light, and moderate temperatures.

Unfortunately, my experiences in the garden have been less successful than those in the lab. I have trouble coaxing them to climb, and seeing naked bamboo stakes in midsummer is frustrating. They grow well enough, but even if I tie them, I don't get the vigor I was expecting. Other problems are also inherent. Rain causes messy spots on the flowers, thus reducing their usefulness. And as hard as I try to deny it, the leaves stink. This is more of a problem if you are handling the plants (e.g., cutting to bring stems indoors), but the wet

Oxypetalum caeruleum

dog smell is not one of its most endearing assets. After flowering, plants produce long boat-shaped green seed pods.

Place plants in full sun, in an area protected from heavy rainfall. I truly love the flowers; I am just not sure how to love the plant.

'Heavenborn' was developed as a cut flower variety and has more vigor than the species. A better choice than the species.

Propagation
Plants are easily propagated by seed.

Method of climbing
Plants produce twining stems but must be tied to get them going.

Etymology
Oxypetalum, from the Greek, *ŏxys* ("sharp") and *petalum* ("petal"), referring to the pointed flower petals; *caeruleum*, dark blue. Tweedia honors John Tweedie, botanist and head gardener at the Royal Botanic Garden in Edinburgh, Scotland, during the mid nineteenth century.

Pandorea (pan-dor′ee-a)
bower vine
Bignoniaceae

Any time you see something in the bignonia family, you can almost be assured that the flowers will be bodacious and the plant will have minimal hardiness. As with everything, there are exceptions, but with this genus, vines will not be perennial unless you live on the Gulf Coast or southern California. In zone 7b, you might get away with plants if they are well protected and heavily mulched. They will take short bursts of 28F, but consistent temperatures below freezing will kill them.

Pandorea jasminoides. Photo by Robert Bowden.

That being said, the most available species, *Pandorea jasminoides*, bower vine, will flower the first year and therefore can be enjoyed in temperate climates, even if plants won't leap tall buildings, and flowers don't appear until well into the season. Of course, they also can be brought indoors for the winter.

Bower vine plants are coveted as much for the glossy green pinnately compound leaves as for the large tubular flowers. The leaves generally have five to nine leaflets, and given time, the plants will branch and produce a full plant, not one with naked legs. The showy five-lobed flowers are 2 to 4 inches long, white on the outside and pink within. In general, they are borne in two- or three-flowered inflorescences. Each flower persists for a short time, but flowers are formed over many months. I read about their fragrance, but I may be nasally challenged as I don't really catch much perfume.

Plants require full sun and lots of water to get started, but once growing, they are surprisingly drought tolerant.

'Alba' has pure white flowers.

'Lady Di' bears white flowers with a creamy throat.

'Rosea' produces pink flowers with a deeper pink throat.

'Rosea Superba' has larger flowers than 'Rosea' and some purple spotting on the petals.

Other species and cultivars

Although bower vine is the easiest to find of the six or so species, all native to eastern Australia and the Pacific Rim, occasionally I see wonga-wonga vine, *Pandorea pandorana*, offered. Plants may be worth buying for the name alone; however, since it blooms on old wood, it will not bloom unless it is brought in during the winters. The flowers are more tubular than those of bower vine; 'Golden Showers' has yellow and red blossoms.

Propagation

Plants can be raised from seeds or from semi-hardwood cuttings in midsummer.

Method of climbing

Plants produce twining stems but must be tied to get them going.

Etymology

Pandorea, named for the beautiful Pandora, of Greek mythology, whom Zeus sent to earth to punish Prometheus, who had stolen fire from heaven. With her, Pandora had a jar (which is today referred to as a box), which she was not to open under any circumstance. However, open it she did. She hastened to close the lid, but all the evil contained therein escaped and spread over the earth, except for one thing which lay at the bottom, and that was Hope; *jasminoides*, resembling jasmine. Bower vine, for their vigorous ability to climb; wonga-wonga, English translation of an Australian Aboriginal word.

Parthenocissus (par-the-no-sis′us)

Virginia creeper

Vitaceae

Nondescript flowers, inconspicuous fruit, and often rampant growth describe plants in the genus, yet their popularity is such that they are in everyday parlance. The ivy-covered walls of Fenway Park, the Ivy League schools, and so many old ivy-covered buildings are all misnamed—but creeper-covered just doesn't have the same romance to it. About ten species are known; two are used all the time, and a couple of others for ornamental purposes.

Parthenocissus quinquefolia (kwin-ke-fo′lee-a)

Virginia creeper

zones 3–9

This American native is a wonderfully tough, almost indestructible vine for walls and buildings. However, make no mistake, it creeps quickly and adheres like Krazy Glue to any rough surface. This is the "ivy" of universities and walls so common in New England.

Parthenocissus quinquefolia, obscuring view somewhat

The leaves consist of five leaflets each attached with a short (¹⁄₃ inch) stalk; light brown stems can grow 6 feet in a year and easily extend to 30 feet in length over time. Small black berries are formed in late summer but are visible only after the leaves have fallen, and only if the birds have not eaten them.

People complain about the stickiness of the tendrils. Their cement-like properties are attachments to help the plant climb and happily adhere to walls of brick or stucco. However, the plants are difficult if not impossible to dislodge from the walls without taking some of the wall with them. From experience, I can tell you stucco is not a good surface to cover with Virginia creeper. However, if you decide the wall will always look better clothed in creeper, then you can be sure your grandkids will enjoy your efforts.

Parthenocissus tricuspidata (tri-kus-pi-da′ta)

Japanese ivy, Boston ivy
zones 4–8

Native to Asia, the vine is so ubiquitous in the Northeast that it has taken on the name of one of our great cities. Plants differ from the native species by having simple leaves rather than compound, and they are a bit shinier as well.

Parthenocissus tricuspidata

The leaves, however, consist of three pointed lobes and are more serrated than the native. Plants may have wonderful burgundy fall color. They are used similarly to *Parthenocissus quinquefolia*, although they perhaps are not quite as hardy.

'Beverley Brook' has larger leaves and good fall color.

'Fenway Park' has bright chartreuse leaves.

'Green Showers' has lustrous leaves larger than the species.

'Purpurea' bears burgundy leaves throughout the summer.

Other species

Parthenocissus henryana, silvervein creeper, is the most ornamental of the group. The young leaves are purple on the underside with a lustrous green color above, intersected with silver veins. As the foliage matures, the intensity of color fades, but plants maintain the silver venation throughout the summer. I really enjoy seeing this plant; unfortunately, the color does not hold in the heat, and plants are cold hardy only to about zone 7.

Parthenocissus henryana.
Photo by Vincent Simeone.

Propagation

Easy to root in the summer with warm (72F) soil temperature and consistent moisture. A low dose of rooting hormone may help uniformity. Plants can be raised from seeds or from semi-hardwood cuttings in midsummer.

Method of climbing

Plants have sticky glue-like tendrils that attach freely. This one is definitely a self-climber.

Etymology

Parthenocissus, from the Greek, *parthenos* ("virgin") and *kissos* ("ivy"), suggesting the English vernacular name; *henryana*, in honor of Augustine Henry (1857–1930), Irish plant collector and dendrologist; *quinquefolia*, five leaves; *tricuspidata*, three-pointed, for the lobes. Virginia creeper, plants are native into Virginia; ivy, resembles ivy in appearance and vigor.

Passiflora (pass-i-flor′a)
passion fruit
Passifloraceae

Everyone has heard of passion fruit, but only a few species are known to gardeners, particularly in temperate zones. From the magnificent maypop (*Passiflora incarnata*) adorning old fence rows in the South to sweet granadilla (*P. ligularis*), whose fruits are eaten raw or used to flavor drinks, to the story of the crucifixion, this genus has it all. The problem with discussing passion vines is where to start. There are so many species (as many as 500 by some counts), let alone cultivars and hybrids, that it is confusing and well-nigh impossible at times to know what to choose. Passion vines have been grown for centuries but all too often by fanciers or in collections few people see. Most garden plants are grown for the flowers, a few for the fruit, but there are some such as bat-leaf passion vine, *P. coriacea*, and *P. boenderi*, whose leaves are the main point of interest.

The ability to find garden plants has become much easier with the advent of the Internet. I visited a number of online retailers and was impressed with the range and diversity of offerings. Grassy Knoll Exotic Plants (www.gkexoticplants.com) in Oregon City, Oregon, offers over 120 taxa, and other sites provide plenty of choice.

Nearly all species are native to South America; a few such as *Passiflora incarnata* and *P. lutea* are North American. A few are sufficiently cold hardy to be considered perennial north to zone 6 (*P. incarnata*, *P. lutea*, *P. caerulea*, and a few hybrids), but the majority are annuals in temperate zones and can be brought in over the winter. They all require well-drained soils, as much sun as possible, and lots of room. Prune out old and weak stems every spring.

Passiflora caerulea (se-rul′ee-a)
blue passion vine
zones 6–9

This is probably the most common passion vine available to gardeners. Although plants are native to Brazil and Argentina, they are among the most reliable for temperate gardeners. They can grow 20 feet in a season, easily covering arbors and trellises. Plants produce deep green leaves (usually palmately five-lobed, but occasionally seven- or nine-lobed), and the large flowers carry tints of white, blue, and purple. The 4-inch-wide flowers, which appear over a long period of the season, only open in the sun and then, if conditions are right, will produce orange egg-shaped fruit.

'Constance Elliott' has bright white flowers.

'Grandiflora' has even larger flowers than the species, sometimes expanding 6 inches across.

Passiflora coccinea (kok-sin'ee-a)
red passion vine
annual

I have seen flowers and plants only in conservatories, but given warm summers, this can do just fine outdoors as well. The oblong leaves are finely pubescent above, quite hairy below, and somewhat leathery. The flowers are up to 6 inches wide, and the petals and sepals are scarlet throughout. Within the flower, the filaments are pale pink to

Passiflora caerulea.
Photo by Alan Shapiro.

Passiflora caerulea,
habit. Photo by Suzy Bales.

white at the base and deep purple toward the top. Plants are eye-catching and quite popular because of the blooms.

Passiflora coriacea (kor-ee-aye' see-a)
bat-leaf passion vine
annual

This is probably one of the most sought-after passion vines because of the leaf shape and common name. The yellow-green flowers bear ivory-colored filaments, but they are rather small, about 1½ inches wide, and generally tucked into the leaf axils. They are handsome but not worth writing home about.

The leaves, on the other hand, are quite different from most other passion vines. They are up to 10 inches long and about 3 inches wide, with essentially entire margins and an obvious midvein. The leaf appears to consist of two joined leaves, but that is not the case. The petiole joins in the middle of the leaf, and the entire leaf is referred to as peltate.

Other species and cultivars
There are so many from which to choose. Here are some I enjoy.

Passiflora ×*alatocaerulea* (syn. *P.* ×*belotii*) is one of the most common and

Passiflora coccinea.
Photo by Alan Shapiro.

Passiflora coriacea.
Photo by Alan Shapiro.

easily obtained hybrids, a cross between *P. caerulea* and *P. alata*. The flowers are lavender with a hint of pink and have long, deep purple stamens; they are sterile, so no fruit will occur. They are also a host for the gulf fritillary butterfly, so expect to see a hungry, purple larva or two.

Passiflora ×*allardii* is a hybrid between *P. caerulea* 'Constance Elliott' and *P. quadrangularis*, giant granadilla, two large-flowered parents. The large flowers are mostly white with some purple, and plants are wildly robust.

Passiflora antioquiensis has long tubular, showy, rose-red flowers. The long tube is characteristic of plants that used to be included in the genus *Tacsonia*.

Passiflora biflora is vigorous and bears small yellow and green flowers.

'Lady Margaret', likely a cross between *Passiflora coccinea* and *P. incarnata*, has beautiful large red flowers with long red stamens, each with a white tip.

Passiflora racemosa, red passion flower, is quite vigorous and, unlike many species, bears flowers in terminal racemes, not singly. The starlike flowers are rich scarlet with purple filaments.

'Sunburst' has small interesting flowers colored in bright orange-yellow. The foliage is also unique, and even when not in flower this hybrid is a handsome plant.

Passiflora ×*alatocaerulea*.
Photo by Judy Laushman.

Passiflora biflora.
Photo by Alan Shapiro.

Propagation

May be propagated by seeds or by terminal cuttings. A low dose of rooting hormone may help uniformity.

Method of climbing

Plants are self-climbers, with long tendrils arising at the axils.

Etymology

Passiflora, from the Latin, *passio* ("passion") and *flos* ("flower"), in reference to Christ's passion; *caerulea*, dark blue; *coccinea*, scarlet; *coriacea*, thick and tough, leathery. Passion flower, the ten colored parts of the floral envelope were thought by early Spanish and Italian travelers to South America to represent the apostles present at the crucifixion, Peter and Judas being absent. Inside the corolla is a showy crown or corona of colored filaments or fringes, taken to represent the crown of thorns, or by some thought to be emblematic of the halo. The stamens are five, suggesting the five wounds, by others thought to be emblematic of the hammers that were used to drive the three nails, the latter being represented by three styles with capitate stigmas. The long axillary coiling tendrils represent the cords or the scourges. The digitate leaves suggest the hands of the persecutors (adapted from Bailey, *Standard Cyclopedia of Botany*, 1944).

Passiflora 'Lady Margaret'. Photo by Alan Shapiro.

Passiflora 'Sunburst'

Periploca (per-i-ploe′ka)

Asclepiadaceae

I had never heard of this genus until I planted something without a label in the Trial Gardens at UGA. It started growing quite slowly and was almost invisible for a year or two, sending up a few shoots with a few leaves. Eventually it did grow and was topping our 8-foot fence and throwing out many stems from the base. It turned out to be silk vine, *Periploca graeca*, a plant native to southern Europe but perfectly hardy all the way to New York State. Plants are woody but entirely deciduous.

It covered an entire section of the fence, but nevertheless, the thing I noticed most was that it crept away from its planting space and popped up in flower beds 5 to 10 feet away. This was not a good thing! The starry five-petaled flowers were quite handsome but visible only on close inspection: they were quite small and quite purple, losing themselves inside the cloak of dark green leaves. In order to see them, you have to get pretty close, and then you can also smell them, not a pleasant smell, and notice their stickiness as well. One thing we also noted was the near absence of fruit, which are quite common under native conditions.

We debated the usefulness of the vine. We were not impressed with the small flowers and did not like the milky sap that oozed from each cut stem, but mostly, we simply tired of digging out the runners. We removed most of it, but some remnants remain. In my view, it is a fine vine, but it could not compete with other more ornamental vines for our limited space.

Periploca graeca. Photo by Meg Green.

Chinese silk vine, *Periploca sepium*, is also occasionally available. It is similar to *P. graeca* but with narrower foliage and is said to be less vigorous.

Propagation

The easiest way is to divide the runners when they occur. Plants can be raised from seeds or terminal cuttings in spring as well.

Method of climbing

Plants need support to get started. After a few years the stems seem to intertwine with each other, but random stems need to be tied to stay up.

Etymology

Periploca, from the Greek, *peˇri* ("around") and *pleˇokoˉ* ("twisted," "woven"); *graeca*, Greek. Silk vine, for the silky seeds that protrude from the open fruit.

Petrea (pet-ray′a)
purple wreath
Verbenaceae

About ten species are known, but the best is *Petrea volubilis*, which has to be one of the most beautiful vines I have seen. It is by no means well known or popular, however, plants are reasonably available online. They are quite woody, so flowers will not occur the first year; therefore, they are useful as perennials only for gardeners in the Gulf Coast and southern California. However, even given these constraints, they are well worth a try.

The opposite leaves are about 8 inches long and 4 inches wide, dark green above, lighter green and slightly hairy beneath. The flowers are really neat. At first glance, the flowers look double, or like blue "hose-in-hose" blossoms. However, look closely, and you first see the five purple radiating starlike sepals and in the center the tubular purple corolla (petals). Dozens of flowers are arranged in 12- to 14-inch-long racemes from late spring to fall. Place in full

Petrea volubilis

Petrea volubilis 'Alba'.
Photo by Alan Shapiro.

sun in well-drained soils. Plants are susceptible to verbena-like problems, especially mealybugs and aphids, so bad at times that a friend who grows one in a greenhouse considers it a mealybug magnet.

Some references suggest plants can't take temperatures below 50F, but I have seen them survive 28F for some time. A few gardeners grow it in more tropical zones, and it probably could survive zone 8/9 winters, with a little protection. However, they certainly are better conservatory plants in temperate zones and need to be planted in large containers and brought in for the winter almost everywhere else.

There is a white-flowered form, 'Alba', as well, but in my opinion, it is not as ornamental.

Propagation
Layering (simple or air) is useful, but semi-hardwood cuttings can also be rooted in moist sand around 72F.

Method of climbing
Plants need support to get started. They are twining plants and will climb through support and other stems.

Etymology
Petrea, for young Lord Robert James Petre (1713–1742), English horticulturist and owner of one of the best private collections of exotics in Europe; *volubilis*, twining. Purple wreath, for the long, flowering racemes.

Phaseolus (fay-ze-o' lus)
bean
Fabaceae

Beans are seldom thought of as particularly ornamental—tasty perhaps, but hardly something you would grow on your arbor. However, I still remember walking to the porch of my brother and sister-in-law's home in Hudson, Quebec, where scarlet runner beans (*Phaseolus coccineus*) were scrambling up the lattice work of their trellis. I was as much a rookie gardener as Mike and Sandi were, and I exclaimed out loud, "Who in their right mind would grow beans by the front door?" Each time I returned those darn beans were prettier and prettier, and mostly I remember the red and white flowers dangling down from the leaves.

I think back to those days—it was the beginning of my appreciation that vegetables could be ornamental. There were many more veggies that are far

Phaseolus coccineus. Photo by Suzy Bales.

more ornamental than this lowly bean, but such memories should be saved. The three leaflets are opposite in arrangement, and each leaflet is about 5 inches long. The flowers actually are scarlet with white wings and keels and are held in a long raceme; the inflorescence is in fact longer than the leaves. The beans are usually 9 to 12 inches and contain black seeds. Plants do best in cool nights and full sun.

Propagation

Save the seeds and store them in a cool, dry place; sow them directly in the ground after the soil warms up, or sow them indoors about two weeks before the frost-free date.

Method of climbing

Plants are twiners, needing something to twist around.

Etymology

Phaseolus, from the Greek, *phasēlŏs* ("bean"); *coccineus*, scarlet.

Podranea (po-dran′ee-a)

Bignoniaceae

You may not have seen a lot of them, but one species of this genus of tropical vines is really quite spectacular: *Podranea ricasoliana*, pink trumpet vine, which you'll likely find only online. Plants are native to South Africa and are annuals in most parts of this country; however, since they flower on new wood, they will flower the first year in the ground, although likely not until September or October. The compound leaves consist of five to eleven leaflets, each one 1 to 2 inches long and with a smooth margin. The large, 2½-inch-long flowers are held in many-flowered inflorescences and are a beautiful pale pink color and pleasantly fragrant. To me, they closely resemble the flowers of Chinese foxglove, *Rehmannia*, or foxgloves themselves. Occasionally, they are striped red inside.

The flowers are similar to other members of the family (*Campsis*, *Bignonia*, *Pandorea*) in that they are big, bold, and colorful. Some people complain that the flowering time is so late, it is not worth giving up so much garden space. Even if it does not command the best place in the garden, once it starts flowering, it will be noticed.

Where perennial, vines can grow 20 feet tall and equally wide, but certainly not half that size if they are treated as annuals. There was a wonderful specimen growing at the State Botanical Garden of Georgia (zone 7b). It was about 7 feet tall and 6 feet around, but to be assured of survival, it was brought indoors during the winter. Full sun is required.

Podranea ricasoliana

Podranea ricasoliana, habit

Propagation

By seeds or from semi-hardwood terminal cuttings. Plants may also root on their own, and these layers can be transplanted elsewhere.

Method of climbing

Plants produce long canes that must be trained to a large structure.

Etymology

Podranea, an anagram of *Pandorea*, the genus with which it was once lumped; *ricasoliana*, in honor of Vincenzo Ricasoli (1814–1891), Italian patron of horticulture. Looks like a trumpet vine, albeit a pink one.

Polygonum (poe-lig′o-num)
    knotweed
    Polygonaceae

This is sometimes called the "mile a minute" vine, as that is how fast it seems to grow once established. I have seen it act like kudzu, dripping and draped from trees and shrubs in the South, but in Niagara Falls in Canada, it is reasonably well behaved. Still, I am not sure I would recommend it for many gardeners. Nearly all plants sold today are *Polygonum aubertii* (silver lace vine, fleece vine).

Plants can easily grow 30 feet tall once established and can also reseed with abandon. The wavy ovate to lanceolate leaves are 2 to 3 inches long, but when the plant flowers, usually in late summer, thousands of plumelike white, bell-shaped flowers are formed in the axils and at the ends of the stems, absolutely covering the plant. When I talk to people, most comments are quite positive, but they all say it must be cut back hard every year and the structure it is growing on must be strong (a brick outhouse is often mentioned).

Plants can be trained to run along fences and up and over arbors. Plants are perfectly cold hardy to zone 5 but are deciduous in the winter. Pedestrians, be warned: this plant has small, rough hairs on the stems, and if it a stray stem falls from the arbor, it will probably grab your hair. Time for the trusty Felcos. Place in full sun and reasonably well-drained soils.

Another species, *Polygonum baldschuanicum* (Russian vine), is occasionally sold and is similar in all respects, except for those hairs. It is similarly grown and similarly hardy. Many authorities have recently lumped the two species under this name. Plants seem to keep going back and forth between *Polygonum* and *Persicaria* (and sometimes *Fallopia*). Since the dust hasn't yet settled, I will simply leave the taxonomy alone.

Also, for those of you who didn't quite get that cutting-back thing, it may be of interest to note that plants are Roundup sensitive, but may require numerous applications.

Propagation

By division, hardwood cuttings, or seeds. It is easy enough to dig out stems and transplant immediately.

Method of climbing

Plants climb by twining stems. They will twist around just about anything.

Etymology

Polygonum, from the Greek, *polys* ("many") and either *gŏnŏs* ("offspring," "seed"), in reference to the many seeds produced, or *gŏny* ("knee-joint"), in reference to the swollen, knotty joints of the stems; *aubertii*, after Georges Eleosippe Auber, French missionary from 1895 to 1901 in China, whence he introduced the species into cultivation; *baldschuanicum*, of Baljuan, Turkistan, Central Asia. The flowers are like lace and, in the right light, give off a silver hue.

Polygonum aubertii

Psiguria (si-gur′ee-a)

pygmymelon
Cucurbitaceae

I first saw a representative of this genus at the Niagara Parks Butterfly Conservatory in Ontario. They were grown in containers in the greenhouses and used as a food source for heliconid butterflies. However, as my colleagues were oohing about the swarming butterflies, I was oohing about the plants.

The species I was oohing about was *Psiguria umbrosa*, pygmymelon. There is a good deal of variation within the genus, and other species may be mislabeled or even unknown. These are "sister" plants to *Gurania* (which see), both of which genera grow in the jungles of Central and South America, both of which have been extensively studied for their relationships with a number of butterfly species, and neither of which is a household name in vines.

Psiguria umbrosa. Photo by Loren Hallstrom.

The most ornamental characteristic is the long racemes of five-petaled orange flowers, obviously attractive to more than just people. They are not large, but each inflorescence carries about a dozen of them, opening from base to apex. The individual flowers do not persist for more than a day or so, but additional flowers keep blooming over a long period of time. The cucumber-like leaves may vary from three- to five-lobed to entire. The large leaves are hard to miss—nothing spectacular, but handsome in their own right.

Plants are monoecious, meaning that separate male and female flowers occur on the same plant. If pollinated, the females produce little striped gourds, carrying the many seeds inside their soft shells. People worry about some of these tropical vines becoming too aggressive. They will not overwinter, so they will never be tree eaters, and if kept cut back in the landscape or greenhouse, they will make handsome specimens.

The last thing I said to myself as I left the butterfly conservatory that first day was, "If this is so beautiful, why have I never heard of it?" Of course, my being clueless about plants was nothing new, so I was determined to bring it home and try it in our greenhouses and gardens. The seeds germinated easily, and the plants look like they will be excellent candidates for our pillars and posts. While I don't expect it to grow to its 30-foot potential, I am betting that it will cover our 7-foot trellis before the frost gets it. In order to stimulate more flowers and reduce leaf size, I will place it in high sun areas, even though it is a forest species.

Being in the cucumber family, it is probably going to be filet for many bugs and fungi, but time will tell. After all, what is a gardener to do, ignore it?

Propagation
By division, hardwood cuttings, or seeds. It is easy enough to dig out stems and transplant immediately.

Method of climbing
Plants climb by tendrils, similar to other members of the family.

Etymology
Psiguria, unknown; *umbrosa*, shade-loving.

Quisqualis (kwis-kwa'lis)
Rangoon creeper
Combretaceae

I first saw one of these weird plants with the wonderful name at the terrific Mercer Arboretum and Botanical Gardens in Humble, Texas. I have since seen *Quisqualis indica* occasionally in other Texas gardens, in Florida, and recently at the conservatory at Longwood. The generic and common names are reason enough to try out this tropical vine in the garden.

Plants are climbers, producing long stems that clothe arches, pillars, and pergolas, and even climb trees. The 7- to 8-inch-long, 3-inch-wide opposite leaves are usually entire and pointed at the tip and held by a 2-inch-long petiole. Of course, it isn't the leaves that people notice but rather the 4-inch drooping inflorescences, consisting of up to a dozen 3-inch-long tubular flowers. The tubes are long and narrow, forming five petal lobes at the end. Each fragrant flower usually opens white then changes to pink or pale red over time. The flowers are formed in the axils as well as terminally, so flowering continues for a long time. The resulting dry leathery fruit is also quite interesting, acutely five-angled and containing a single seed.

Plants are native to Malaysia and Southeast Asia and will not overwinter in temperate gardens. They may survive to about zone 8b with protection. In the Houston area, where freezes occur, plants may die to the ground, but they come back fine the next year, growing to about 15 feet. Not something for everyone, but if a warm garden or heated conservatory is looking for a vine to fill some space, the Rangoon creeper may be just the ticket.

Propagation

From softwood cuttings during the summer or seed. Seed-propagated plants may take on a bushy habit when young, before sending out long scandent branches.

Method of climbing

They may be tied, but as growth occurs, they will twine around themselves.

Etymology

Quisqualis, lots of interesting stories as to the origin—one account suggests the Latin *quis* ("who?") and *qualis* ("what?") was given by German botanist G. E. Rumphius, in astonishment over the plant's behavior. He told of how the plant grows as a shrub up to 3 feet, then throws out new growth from the base that climbs up neighboring trees, after which the original shrub dies; *indica*, of India, but also applied to plants originating throughout the East Indies and as far away as China. Rangoon creeper, Rangoon is probably from the British imitation of the former capital of Burma (Myanmar), Yangon.

Quisqualis indica

Quisqualis indica,
habit

Rhodochiton (row-doe-ki'ten)

purple bells

Scrophulariaceae

You can sometimes walk by *Rhodochiton atrosanguineus* and not even see the flowers. They are so purple, they blend in with the dark foliage. The fact that they are pendulous and somewhat hidden by the leaves may also explain the oversight. The 3-inch-long heart-shaped leaves, held on long petioles, are pale green and a little darker green above, but never particularly lustrous. Plants are particularly useful in hanging baskets.

The flowers are really quite lovely if you take the time to look at them. The five-lobed reddish calyx is about 2 inches wide and looks like a wide-brimmed hat shading the rest of the flower. Hanging from the calyx is the long tubular blood-red to purple petal tube, flaring to five obvious lobes. Within the petals are tucked the four white stamens. After pollination, the petals will fall away, but the sepals will expand and turn greenish to rose-red and remain on the plant for a long time. All in all, a beautifully packaged and handsome flower.

That it is only cold hardy to about zone 8 limits its popularity; however, since it grows 10 to 12 feet in a single season, it should not be limited too much. Provide plenty of sun, but in the South, provide afternoon shade as well. In the North, full sun is fine. Plants are native to sandy soils in Mexico; therefore, do not place in heavy clay soils if possible.

Rhodochiton atrosanguineus

Propagation
From seed. Fresh seed germinates faster and more uniformly than older seed.

Method of climbing
The petioles twist around, a little like those of *Clematis*.

Etymology
Rhodochiton, from *rhŏdŏ* ("red") and *chitōn* ("cloak"), in reference to the long reddish calyx; *atrosanguineus*, not just red, but dark, blood-red. Purple bells, from the dark pendulous flowers.

Rosa (roze′a)
rose
Rosaceae

I am sitting here scratching my head, wondering where to start with this incredibly large group of plants. I have always resisted growing roses because of the troubles with virus, black spot, mildew, caterpillars, and Lord knows what else. I have always enjoyed roses in other peoples' gardens, knowing that they were doing all the work. Nor have I ever been a fan of rose gardens, but I surely do enjoy shrub roses in the perennial or shrub garden.

As I garden more, I have felt the pull to try more roses. When I finally moved to a house with a garden with sufficient light, I decided to stick my big toe in the rose ocean, and I have come around to their lure and appeal, without getting too carried away. I have a few more than I did ten years ago. Heaven help me, however, if I lose it all and join a rose society. Rosarians are nothing if not passionate, and—without doubt—between trading, sharing, and photo-drooling, I would soon be awash in the things. I have no doubt a rosarian is right now checking out this chapter, likely at a library or bookstore (so he doesn't have to buy the book), to be sure I have not written anything unkind about his beloved babies.

I have seen beautiful climbers and ramblers in gardens all over the world. If nothing else, the performance of roses is as influenced by local heat, humidity, cold, snow, and bugs as any group of plants I have ever tried. So while I take notes in gardens around the world, I listen to local gardeners far more than I do to catalogs. Good grief, is there a single bad photo of any rose in catalogs?

Since I am but a rookie at the rose game, I wanted a few answers to my climbing questions. First of all, what in the world is the difference between a rambler and a climber? I went to the American Rose Society (www.ars.org), various gardeners, growers, and books, and could find nothing particularly consistent. It turns out that climbers have larger flowers in smaller trusses and (at least in the modern selections) generally flower more than once (they are remontant). Ramblers (such as 'American Pillar') have more flexible canes and are easier to train on pergolas and other structures; they generally flower only once a season. Not much to stick to your ribs, but it seems that if you are looking for a climbing rose, you have sufficient choices. By the way, 'New Dawn' is the archetypal climber, the insidious *Rosa multiflora*, the archetypal rambler.

Pruning of climbers, of course, is always a question that arises whenever roses are discussed. I dusted off my old rose book, read the instructions, looked at the drawings of the three or four stems pruned into a neat fan, and with soaring confidence took out my trusty Felcos, ready to get to work. As I surveyed my 'New Dawn' roses, I was immediately transported to a Disney scene, the one where the prince arrives at the castle where Sleeping Beauty is being held by the wicked witch. The prince comes to the walls of the castle, covered to depths of ten feet or more with a sharp, dense thicket of brambles. That's what greeted me when I went out to assert control of my vines. The prince had more magic in his shears than I had in mine, and after a brief but

Rosa 'American Pillar' at Longwood Gardens

bloody foray into the thicket, I went back to those drawings, ripped them up, and had a beer.

Now, I simply keep the roses from eating the house, growing through the deck, or intimidating my grandkids. I contacted a couple of friends who love and grow many climbers. One was Mike Shoup, the owner of Antique Rose Emporium in Brenham, Texas, and the other was Suzy Bales, a rose expert on Centre Island, New York. I love them both, and particularly I was taken by how Suzy answered when someone asked her about the intricacies of pruning: "Ah, just cut them back whenever, and wherever, you can—there are no rules." Thank you, Suzy. Both Mike and Suzy provide a list of their favorite roses, later on.

Nearly all climbers are grown on their own roots, thus eliminating problems of bud union, wild rootstock taking over, and lack of cold hardiness of the bud union. They all need as much sun as you can provide regardless of any claims of shade tolerance. Most flower in spring and, if cut back, may flower again well into the late summer and fall. As with clematis, hundreds of hybrids and selections of climbing roses are available. Whatever you choose, I agree with Suzy Bales: "Climbers have to be able to care for themselves with

Rosa 'New Dawn'. Photo by Suzy Bales.

only minimum care. I provide compost once a year and weekly watering, and prune out the dead when I see it. I do not use chemical fertilizers or pesticides, nor do I prune back until they have run out of room to climb or are heading in the wrong direction." No wonder I love this woman!

Species and cultivars

Most climbing roses sold today are hybrids of some sort, providing exceptional vigor with an endless array of flower colors and types, but two species are still reasonably easy to obtain.

Rosa banksiae from China, otherwise known as Lady Banks' rose, is my favorite species rose. The common form has small double yellow flowers; this *R. banksiae* 'Lutea', as she is properly known, shows up on many Top Ten lists of climbing roses. I love her vigor—she eventually climbs to 20 feet if allowed. I love her thornless habit—a rose I can finally hug. I love the hundreds of double yellow flowers in the spring. The flowers have hardly any fragrance, and unfortunately, plants are cold hardy only to about zone 7, but she is terrific. A double white ('Alba Plena'), a single white (var. *normalis*), and a single yellow ('Lutescens') have all been introduced, and all have more fragrant flowers than the common double-flowered form.

Rosa laevigata is the opposite of Lady Banks' rose in many ways: it has many more stems, awful hooked thorns, and single, white fragrant flowers. Plants are native to China; they were introduced to the American South around 1780

Rosa laevigata

and became naturalized quickly. Now known as the Cherokee rose, it became the state flower of Georgia. Hardy to zone 7 only.

The criteria for "best" changes, depending on the person giving them. To select "best" cultivars, I talked to many people and looked at comments on the Internet. In so doing, I noticed that a few received ringing endorsements from many individuals and groups, North to South. Here are a few of the consensus winners. Many were named in the Top Ten of climbing roses by more than one source (and turn up again in Mike and Suzy's select lists). Remember to talk to local gardeners for the best ones in your area; they may not even be listed here.

Pink. Belle of Portugal (= 'Belle Portugaise'), 'Bubble Bath', 'Climbing Cécile Brünner', 'Climbing Pink', 'Cornelia', 'Jeanne Lajoie', 'New Dawn', Pierre de Ronsard (= 'Meiviolin'), 'William Baffin', 'Zéphirine Drouhin'.

Yellow/apricot. 'Abraham Darby', 'America', 'Autumn Sunset', 'Buff Beauty', 'Buff Yellow', 'Golden Showers', 'Graham Thomas', 'Royal Sunset', 'Westerland'.

Rosa 'Climbing Pink' in the Trial Gardens at UGA

Red. Altissimo (= 'Delmur'), 'Blaze', 'Don Juan', 'Dortmund', 'Dublin Bay', 'Fourth of July'.

Rosa 'Zéphirine Drouhin'.
Photo by Richard Warren.

White. 'City of York', 'Iceberg', 'Madame Alfred Carrière', 'Sally Holmes', 'Sombreuil'.

The preceding roses may be a good place to start, but to save us all some time, I asked Mike and Suzy to name their top climbers and tell why they make the cut.

Mike Shoup's Top Climbing Roses. "I like 'Crepescule' and 'Madame Alfred Carrière' (fragrant, repeat-blooming vigorous varieties, both noisettes). I also enjoy 'Lavender Lassie' and 'Prosperity' (hybrid musks); 'Climbing Souvenir de la Malmaison' (bourbon); 'Climbing Cécile Brünner' (sweetheart polyantha); and 'Sombreuil' (syn. 'Colonial White'), probably a wichuraiana hybrid. All are my favorites. 'Climbing American Beauty' and 'Veilchenblau' are worth mentioning; although they are spring bloomers, they are very dramatic."

Suzy Bale's Top Climbing Roses. "'New Dawn' leads my list. Pointy buds open to double blush-pink flowers with slight apple fragrance, if you stick your nose right in it. It is a tall grower (10 to 15 feet), and the flowers are good for cutting, too.

'Aloha' is the best of the climbing hybrid teas with a strong tea rose fragrance. Its dark green, leathery leaves set off abundant rosy pink, cupped flowers fully packed with up to sixty petals. Each petal is darker on the outside than the inside. The climber grows 7 to 10 feet and is easy to keep inbounds. I frequently cut the flowers for bouquets.

'Dublin Bay' is the best climbing red. It grows up to 12 feet high and has delightfully fragrant velvety blooms that keep coming all summer and long into the fall. The blooms are made for bouquets.

Rosa 'Buff Beauty'

Rosa 'New Dawn'

'William Baffin' bears semi-double, deep pink flowers and climbs up to 10 feet high. I have it growing on the pillar of the porch, where we frequently eat in the summer. We admire its beauty up close daily. It was bred in Canada and is cold hardy to zone 3.

'Climbing Cécile Brünner' grows up to 20 feet high and almost as wide if left to its own devices. Each thimble-sized pink bud and rose is a perfect miniature of a hybrid tea rose, lightly scented; they bloom in clusters of a dozen or more. Mine covers one side of the house, clinging to the ivy as it climbs.

'Dortmund' is a single-flowered beauty with red petals that open to white eyes and yellow stamens—striking color combination, indeed. If I didn't know better, I might expect them to blink. If they are deadheaded after their first all-out bloom, the flowers keep coming. Its foliage is tough and shiny and not susceptible to disease. Exceptionally cold hardy and long lived."

Propagation
Roses can be increased by terminal cuttings.

Rosa 'William Baffin'.
Photo by Suzy Bales.

Rosa 'Aloha'. Photo by
Suzy Bales.

Rosa 'Dortmund'. Photo
by Suzy Bales.

Method of climbing
All roses need tying to get started. They will grow through other stems.

Etymology
Rosa, the Latin name for rose; *banksiae*, for Lady Dorothea Banks (1758–1828), wife of Sir Joseph Banks; *laevigata*, smooth.

Schizophragma (skiz-o-frag′ma)
climbing hydrangea
Hydrangeaceae

Climbing hydrangeas were always favorite vines of mine growing up in Canada; however, it seems that there, as well as in this country, there was some confusion between two species of *Schizophragma*, also known as hydrangea vines, and the true climbing hydrangea, *Hydrangea anomala* ssp. *petiolaris*. All have the same climbing habit, all are vigorous but take a number of years before they really flower well, and all are better plants in the North than the South. Members of both genera are most easily recognized by the large, showy sterile flowers that surround the 8- to 10-inch-wide clusters of lacecap-like flowers. In *Hydrangea*, this encircling halo is made up of greenish white flowers, each actually four rounded sepals; in *Schizophragma*, the 1- to 1½-inch-wide sepals are often a purer white and are borne singly rather than in fours. Here are a few other differences, for slow learners like me:

Schizophragma	*Hydrangea a.* ssp. *petiolaris*
Leaves barely rounded at base, coarsely toothed,	Leaves heart-shaped, finely toothed,
lower surface much lighter in color than veins	lower surface same color as veins
Bark firm	Bark shredding

It is also useful to note that schizophragmas often bloom a little later, their sepals remain showy longer into the season, and all in all, they are neater and arguably showier plants than true climbing hydrangeas. Plants are particularly effective growing up a large rough-barked tree (like an oak) or along a fence line.

Schizophragma hydrangeoides, Japanese hydrangea vine, is an excellent, vigorous species. Two of its selections are worth mentioning: 'Moonlight' has silvery, blue-green foliage that is quite handsome but fades once established; 'Roseum' has rose-flushed sepals. Also fine and even more vigorous is *S. integrifolium*, Chinese hydrangea vine. At Chanticleer, in Wayne, Pennsylvania, this is a spectacular vine in the month of June; the sterile flowers are creamy white and the leaves are larger and lighter green than those of *S. hydrangeoides*.

Propagation
From terminal cuttings in late summer.

Method of climbing
Plants have holdfasts like Boston ivy and will cement themselves to any rough structure.

Schizophragma hydrangeoides, habit. Photo by Vincent Simeone.

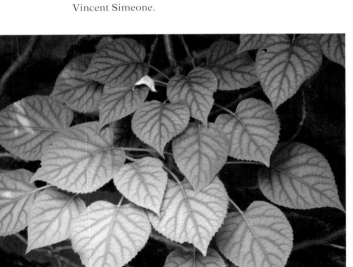

Schizophragma hydrangeoides. Photo by Vincent Simeone.

Schizophragma hydrangeoides 'Moonlight'

Schizophragma hydrangeoides 'Roseum'

Schizophragma integrifolium at Chanticleer

Etymology

Schizophragma, from the Greek, *schizo* ("cut") and *phragma* ("fence," "screen"), because the fruit is divided into two separate parts by the septum of its inner wall; *hydrangeoides*, like an hydrangea; *integrifolium*, entire leaves.

Senecio (sen-ee′ cee-o)
orangeglow vine
Asteraceae

Senecio has the distinction of having the most species in the plant kingdom, somewhere between 2,000 and 3,000. Nearly every form of plant can be found, from annual herbs to shrubs and small trees. Only a half-dozen vining members occur, and only one is easily available. There are but a few daisy-flowered vines in the entire plant kingdom, and this is probably the best known. Plants have been known as *Senecio confusus*, a wonderful name to wonder where the confusion was, but it is now being saddled with the incredibly ugly name of *Pseudogynoxys chenopodioides* by some taxonomists. As for me, I will remain confused until taxonomists agree.

The deep green alternate leaves are narrow, smooth, and with a dentate

Senecio confusus, habit

margin, while the daisy flowers are unique in that they are a bold orange. At the base of the daisies is a small set of bracts known as a pappus, a structure characteristic of all members of the genus. As much as I like this bright vine, the 2-inch-wide flowers are not particularly numerous and do not appear until the fall. This is an easy annual vine to cultivate. I grow it every year, but I think I may do it because I like its name so much. If its name does change, it will be history. Horticulturists have to draw the line somewhere!

Propagation
From seed or by cuttings.

Method of climbing
Plants consist of long stems that need to be tied to remain upright.

Senecio confusus.
Photo by Meg Green.

Etymology
Senecio, from the Latin *senex* ("old man"), for the hairy pappus at the base of the flower; *confusus*, confused, apt to be taken for another species. Orange-glow vine, for the vibrant orange flowers.

Solanum (so-lan'um)
potato vine
Solanaceae

Potato vines are always entertaining, as people wonder where the potatoes are. Think of the confusion with ornamental potatoes out there. We have the sweet potato (*Ipomoea*), with its large edible tuber, the air potato (*Dioscorea*), with "potatoes" hanging from the stems, and the potato vine, with no potatoes at all. No wonder we're all confused. There are over 1,400 species of herbs, shrubs, poisonous plants, and a few vines in this genus. The potato, deadly nightshade, naranjilla, and Jerusalem cherry are but a few of its better-known members.

Some of the potato vines that can be found are generally hardy only to about 20F; others will take no frost at all. They generally have blue to violet flowers that are similar in shape if not in size to those of tomatoes. All prefer full sun and well-drained soils.

Solanum crispum (kris'pum)
Chilean potato vine
zones 8–10

I first saw this plant in England and immediately realized that if it looked that good in Sussex, it would look awful in Athens, Georgia, and dead in Madison, Wisconsin. However, that did nothing to quench my admiration of the plant.

Plants are offered as 'Glasnevin', from the National Botanic Gardens of Ireland in the city of that name. It is a large rambling shrub; some call it a wall plant, because it is often planted on a large trellis at the base of a building. Having said that, I hasten to add it had better be a tough building, because these suckers can grow 30 feet or more and can get there in a few years. The 4- to 5-inch-long lanceolate leaves have wavy margins and are finely hairy beneath. The large violet-blue flowers have yellow centers and are held in small packages of a half-dozen flowers. The stems are not spiny, rather unusual for some of the ornamental members, many of which put a rose to shame.

As with all marginal plants, a good deal of contradiction concerning winter hardiness is out there. With protection, or growing at the base of a wall or building, it may be hardy to zone 7b. In the Pacific Northwest, where milder climates in both winter and summer occur, it is perfectly hardy. Leaving plants outside much further north than zone 8 is a gamble or folly, depending on your pocketbook. Plants can be pruned back and overwintered in a heated (40F) garage under lights. They will be deciduous below zone 8, but evergreen in milder climes.

Full sun or some afternoon shade, acid soil, and out of the prevailing winds seems to help.

Solanum crispum
'Glasnevin'

Solanum crispum
'Glasnevin', habit

Solanum jasminoides (jazz-min-oy'deez)

potato vine

zones 7–9

This is probably the most common potato vine and is also the most cold hardy. Plants are native to Brazil and in some areas, such as southern Florida and Hawaii, have become a noxious weed. However, for the rest of us, it is a wonderfully vigorous vine with bluish, or more commonly, white flowers. The many-branched plants bear many unarmed (thornless) shoots with dark green compound leaves, with three to five ovate leaflets, each one entire and about 2 inches long. They are evergreen as far north as zone 7, but deciduous in cooler climates.

The flowers are borne on short racemes; each 1-inch-wide flower has shallowly five-toothed sepals beneath star-shaped petals. The flowers are white with a bluish tinge with beautiful, contrasting lemon-yellow stamens.

'Album' is the most common selection and often the only one available. The flowers are pure white. Plants are more vigorous and appear to be more cold hardy than the species.

'Variegatum' has yellow and green variegated foliage, and flowers like those of the species. Plants are not as vigorous as 'Album'.

Solanum jasminoides 'Variegatum', habit

Solanum jasminoides
'Album'

Solanum jasminoides
'Variegatum'. Photo by
Alan Shapiro

Solanum wendlandii (wend-land′ee-eye)
   paradise flower
   zones 9–11

I have seen many plants in my day, but I still believe this is one of the most beautiful vines I have ever come across. Perhaps it is because I was wandering around Heronswood Nursery, one of the finest horticulture establishments in Australia, when I first saw it. Perhaps because the owner, writer Clive Blazey, was somewhat nonchalant about it as I went ga-ga. Or, as I think about it, it may have been the subtle red Australian wine I was sipping on the porch. Who cares—it was marvelous there and has been almost as spectacular in the Trial Gardens at UGA.

Plants can grow up to 50 feet in southern California, but 10 to 15 feet is far more common for the rest of us. They bear variably shaped leaves; the most common are the 8- to 10-inch-long compound leaves with a large terminal leaflet and eight to twelve significantly smaller laterals. The stems are reasonably unarmed, but the petioles and the leaf midribs are armed with lethal hooked spines. So be careful: they don't just poke you, they take chunks out of you. Lethal or not, the flowers are well worth the pain.

Flowers are borne on new wood, so even in Chicago, if plants are put out in late spring, the ensuing growth will also provide the flowers. The pale lilac-blue flowers are probably the largest in the genus and are borne in inflorescences up to 8 to 10 inches across. The wonderful individual cuplike flowers are about 2½ inches across and persist for weeks. We have never had the vine loaded with flowers, but once summer warms up, we always have some flowers from July on. Of course, warm summers ensure best growth and flowering, and plants do better in St. Louis, Missouri, than Portland, Maine. However, in Maine, they still grow 3 to 4 feet in summer.

Place in full sun, provide well-drained soils, and fertilize heavily as growth occurs. In general, plants need to be brought in over the winter and placed in a cool, lighted space. Plants take about 28F.

Propagation
Plants are easily increased from cuttings in summer.

Method of climbing
All potato vines need support to get started. They also need tying or other support to keep them upright. Eventually they will twine around themselves.

Etymology
Solanum, Latin name for some plant, probably *S. nigrum*; *crispum*, finely waved, closely curled, referring to the crispate leaf margins; *jasminoides*, resembling *Jasminum*, for the flowers; *wendlandii*, for German botanist Hermann Wendland (1825–1903), who sent this vine to RBG Kew in 1890. Potato vine, for the potato-like flowers.

Solanum wendlandii.
Photo by Meg Green.

Solanum wendlandii,
habit

Sollya (saul′ya)
bluebell creeper
Pittosporaceae

There is probably no good reason to include *Sollya heterophylla* in the book, except that when I don't include something, invariably I will receive complaints from people who wonder how I could omit such a wonderful plant. It is not that I don't like this western Australian species; it simply will not grow in 95 percent of this country and is unavailable in another 4 percent. However, I suppose a few other plants snuck into this book about which the same could be said. I discovered good old "Solly" in Canberra, covering a large corner of Ben and Ros Walcott's garden. Next time you are in Canberra, go see Ben and Ros; they are spectacular people, and their garden is equally nice.

The plant has alternate, simple narrow leaves, and although it can take up a lot of space, it seldom grows more than 6 feet in height. Plants are more elegant than awesome, as the small blue flowers never cover the plant, but nor are they sparsely manufactured. The flowers are formed in many-flowered clusters, each one bell-shaped, less than ½ inch long and dark blue. Decorative fruits follow. Pruning the plant hard results in much better branching and many more stems.

Plants need full sun. They must be brought in if temperatures are below

Sollya heterophylla, flowers and fruit.
Photo by Ben Walcott.

Sollya heterophylla, habit

freezing. They may handle an occasional light freeze, but planting in a large container or tub is recommended so they may be brought in during the winter. They flower on old wood, so plants must be established to see some blooms.

Propagation

Plants are reasonably easy from soft cuttings in spring or early summer. Seed germination is difficult.

Method of climbing

Plants need support to get started and will creep for a while unless help is provided. The long, climbing stems will eventually grow through each other. They also need tying or other support to keep them upright. Eventually they will twine around themselves.

Etymology

Sollya, named for Richard Horsman Solly (1778–1858), English plant physiologist and anatomist; *heterophylla*, diversely leaved. Bluebell creeper, for the bluebell-like flowers and its tendency to creep rather than climb.

Stictocardia (stik-toe-kar′dee-a)

Convolvulaceae

Of the twelve or so species in this genus, my choice is *Stictocardia beraviensis*, probably because it is the only one I can find. It is an excellent screening vine, producing really handsome large (8- to 10-inch) heart-shaped leaves that are densely hairy when young and remain gray-green as they mature. Beneath the leaves you will also likely see some dark glands. As the plant grows, the leaves overlap, and if you want to grab a quick smoke behind it, nobody will see you. Even if they never flowered, they are neat plants to try. I have written about many vines that are less than well known. That they are annual, perhaps don't grow as rapidly as one would like, or have less than overwhelming flowers will forever keep these plants below the radar. Here is another. However, there are some excellent reasons for getting off our collective duffs and getting it into the garden.

The common name, Hawaiian sunset vine, comes from the flashy flowers. As they grow, they produce 2-inch-wide morning glory–like flowers that are coral, crimson, and yellow all at once. I really can't describe them, but people will gather around them. Having made you anticipate such beauty, I must tell you that in most temperate climates, they flower quite sparsely, and the flower stems may not be long enough to allow you to see the flowers without moving a few leaves aside. Nevertheless, any flower on this plant is cause for a stictocardia party. Plants are closely related to *Ipomoea* and have been classified as such in the past. Ipomoeas also have some timid flowerers, like sweet potato vine, so perhaps this characteristic is not too surprising.

We grew *Stictocardia beraviensis* in the Trial Gardens at UGA, and it did soar. Flowers were few, but they were as beautiful as I described. Then I saw its close relative, *S. campanulata*, flowering and strutting its 10-foot height in Chanticleer Garden in Wayne, Pennsylvania, and I knew we had a winner.

Propagation

Plants can be increased by hardwood cuttings in mid to late summer. Seeds germinate readily.

Stictocardia campanulata, flower

Stictocardia campanulata
at Chanticleer

Method of climbing
Stems twine, like morning glory vine.

Etymology
Stictocardia, from the Greek, *stictos* ("spotted") and *kardia* ("heart"), the undersides of the heart-shaped leaves are spotted with glands; *beraviensis*, from Beravi, on the western edge of Madagascar. Hawaiian sunset, for the flamboyant flowers.

Tecomaria (tek-o-mare′ ee-a)
Cape honeysuckle
Bignoniaceae

I debated as to whether one species of this genus, *Tecomaria capensis*, was a vine or a shrub, as many members of this family produce long, arching stems that can be pruned into hedges or shrubs or allowed to ramble and romp. Cape honeysuckle is native to South Africa and produces vibrant orange-red flowers over stems with opposite leaves consisting of seven to nine serrated leaflets.

Plants can grow in freeze-free zones, can climb 20 feet tall, and will flower in fall and winter, into spring. In more northern areas, plants will flower in the late spring and again in the fall. The long tubular flowers are about 2 inches long with four spreading lobes at the end. The color is eye-catching for sure, but do not fertilize heavily, as few flowers will be produced. In freeze-free zones, provide full sun and lots of room. There are many reports that the roots are invasive, so be careful when this is planted in reasonably rich soils.

Tecomaria capensis 'Aurea'. Photo by Robert Bowden.

In the North, bring plants into a cool, bright area during the winter and bring out after the last frost. Not one of my favorite plants, to be sure, but colorful if flowers appear copiously.

'Apricot' has orange flowers and is more compact.

'Aurea' bears yellow blooms.

Propagation
By seed, or by cuttings in spring and summer.

Method of climbing
Climbs with twining stems.

Etymology

Tecomaria, from *Tecoma*, which it closely resembles; *capensis*, of the Cape of Good Hope, South Africa. Cape honeysuckle, the flowers look like those of *Lonicera*, honeysuckle.

Thunbergia (thun-ber'gee-a)
Acanthaceae

Some of the most beautiful flowers can be found on these plants, and while one or possibly two species enjoy a little popularity, it is a genus that too few gardeners are aware of. Unfortunately, none of the species are reliably cold hardy below zone 8, and some not even that. The showy flowers are yellow, blue, or orange and are subtended by two bracts beneath the flowers. The bracts help in distinguishing the genus from others.

Thunbergia alata (a-lat'a)
black-eyed Susan vine
annual

This is by far the best known of the thunbergias, a vigorous vine that flowers throughout the summer and fall. The 3-inch-long triangular leaves are opposite and dentate, with growth on either side of the petiole, referred to as wings. The single yellow-orange flowers have a dark purple-black throat and are subtended by inflated bracts beneath. They occur in the axils of the leaves and will continue all summer in most areas of the country.

This is an easy-to-grow vine and will grow up any structure. It also makes a stunning hanging basket, with such vigor that the basket is essentially invisible. When planting in the ground or a container, place two or three plants together to provide more "body." Full sun and copious water to begin, then leave it alone.

Several breeders are working on this plant, but the majority of the varieties will be shades of colors, and in fact, they are quite similar to each other.

African Sunset mix is a mixture of red, apricot, peach, pink, salmon, and ivory with burgundy eyes.

'Alba' has white flowers with a dark throat.

'Blushing Susie' bears predominantly red flowers, although some flowers will also be in ivory and apricot shades.

Salmon shades are just that.

Thunbergia alata mix
at Al's Garden Center,
Woodburn, Oregon

Thunbergia alata
'Sunny Lemon Star'

Thunbergia alata 'Sunny Orange'

'Spanish Eyes' produces flowers of apricot, salmon, rose, and ivory.

Sunny series includes 'Sunny Lemon Star' and 'Sunny Orange'.

Superstar mix has some of the larger flowers in the species, a vibrant orange with black eyes.

Susie mix, including 'Blushing Susie', bears flowers in white and orange.

Thunbergia grandiflora (gran-di-flor'a)
clock vine
zones 8–10

Probably the prettiest vine in the genus, this plant produces large dark lustrous rough leaves with toothed margins. In addition to the good-looking foliage are the even better looking flowers. The single blooms are large (3 inches across and equally long) and are the most beautiful sky blue to dark blue in color, with white throats.

Thunbergia grandiflora. Photo by Alan Shapiro.

Plants are native to northern India and cannot be expected to be perennial in much of this country. In the Trial Gardens at UGA (zone 7b), the plant came back for about four years, but it was slow to emerge and did not flower until the fall. But how we looked forward to it! There is a white-flowered form, 'Alba', but it is not as pretty as the species. Plants can be overwintered in a cool area with bright light.

Thunbergia grandiflora, habit

Thunbergia grandiflora 'Alba'.
Photo by Alan Shapiro.

Thunbergia gregorii

Thunbergia gregorii (gre-gore'ee-eye)
　　orange clock vine
　　annual

Another beautiful flowering vine, almost totally unknown. The triangular leaves are about 2½ inches long, softly hairy and with toothed margins. The petioles are winged like those of *Thunbergia alata*. The funnel-shaped flowers are almost 2 inches wide and are bright orange and lack the dark eye. Beautiful, just hard to find.

Propagation
By cuttings in the summer.

Method of climbing
Plants twine and curl around structures.

Etymology
Thunbergia, for Swedish botanist Carl Peter Thunberg (1743–1828), who explored South Africa and Japan looking for new plants and later became a professor at Uppsala; *alata*, winged, for the petiole; *grandiflora*, large flowers; *gregorii*, for British geologist and explorer John Walter Gregory (1864–1932), who collected the type specimen. Black-eyed Susan, for the black centers, named for my wife, Susan; clock vine, the stems twist in a clockwise fashion.

Trachelospermum (tray-ke-lo-sper'mum)
　　star jasmine
　　Apocynaceae

It is hard not to want to have one of these plants in your garden when you are surrounded by the fragrance on a cool, still spring evening. This woody vine/groundcover belongs to the same family as *Vinca* and sports similar five-petaled flowers. In this case the flowers are more star-shaped and wonderfully fragrant. Two species are commonly found, the most fragrant and certainly the best is star or confederate jasmine, *Trachelospermum jasminoides*, native to China. This evergreen is usually trained to climb a trellis or fence, but it can also be trimmed into a hedge-like form or allowed to roam as a groundcover. The opposite ovate to rounded leaves are about 1½ inches long and pointed at the tips. They are a lustrous dark green with obvious venation. The white flowers occur in spring and early summer and have a delicious fragrance of jasmine. They grow beautifully in the Founders Garden, the first Garden Club in America, founded 1891, in Athens, but I love these especially in Savannah and Charleston, where they seem to thrive.

Unfortunately, they are consistently cold hardy only to zone 7b; I have seen plants looking good in Raleigh, North Carolina (7a), but a hard winter may take them out if planted too far north. The fragrance is worth planting them in a tub and overwintering indoors if possible. Plant in a sheltered location, in partial shade and away from wind. Prune back hard every year to keep it in bounds. Once established, it can grow rapidly. Be careful: plants exude a white sap to which some people may be allergic.

'Madison' is similar to *Trachelospermum jasminoides* but is said to be slightly more cold hardy. May be a common name for the species.

'Pink Showers', with habit and fragrance similar to the species, has flowers in a nice soft shade of pink.

'Variegatum' has flowers similar to the type but sports white and green foliage.

Other species

Trachelospermum asiaticum, Japanese star jasmine, is also easily found but is not nearly as well behaved. They are more cold hardy, perhaps to zone 6b or 7a, and the flowers are not as clean a white, perhaps a little more yellowish white. Interestingly, they do not flower nearly as prolifically as *T. jasminoides*, in some years not at all. There are more reports of this plant escaping and being quite invasive; my colleague Dr. Tim Smalley would "never recommend it." Plants spread by underground stems and get everywhere. It is far worse than *T. jasminoides*, but both benefit from judicious pruning.

Propagation

By semi-hardwood cuttings in the summer.

Method of climbing

Plants twine and curl around structures. They need tying to get started if using a trellis.

Etymology

Trachelospermum, from the Greek, *trachēlos* ("neck") and *sperma* ("seed"), referring to the extension or "neck" of the seed; *asiaticum*, Asian; *jasminoides*, resembling jasmine in fragrance. Confederate jasmine, due to its popularity in the South; star jasmine, for the shape of the flowers.

Trachelospermum jasminoides, habit

Trachelospermum jasminoides

Trachelospermum jasminoides 'Variegatum'

Tropaeolum (tro-pay-ol'um)
nasturtium
Tropaeolaceae

Historically, nasturtium pods and seeds were used in pickling, and the spicy peppery leaves were sometimes used in salads and became known as Indian cress. There are well over eighty species, and even master gardeners would be hard-pressed to name more than a couple. This is not surprising as I can't think of any frost-tolerant perennial nasturtiums, and the only one most people see is the gaudily-colored bedding forms of *Tropaeolum majus*. However, in my travels here and there, I have been so impressed with some of the climbers that I have bought seed and even tubers of various taxa back to Georgia and given them a go. Unfortunately, I have yet to be overwhelmed with my success, but gardeners are, if nothing else, persistent. If they must be annuals, so be it. If I can reproduce a canary creeper, it will be worth it. I have killed *T. tuberosum* and especially *T. speciosum* to the point of being called a plant molester, so perhaps it is time to move on. However, please feel free to try some of the more difficult forms. After all, it is only money.

Tropaeolum speciosum before I got my hands on it

Tropaeolum majus (may'jus)
common nasturtium
annual

I have seen hundreds upon hundreds of nasturtiums in this country, and most are cool-loving, colorful bedding plants. Vibrant and handsome as they are, I squint, study, and eyeball these little fellows and wonder when they will begin to climb. Of course, most will not: the breeders have selected non-climbing forms as bedding plants. However, choose the proper cultivar and climbers can be enjoyed. But there's a catch—most of the climbers are old-fashioned cultivars and are far more difficult to acquire. In Victorian days, it was common to grow nasturtiums up wigwams of sticks, but that activity is seldom seen these days.

Nevertheless, the plants produce rather handsome orbicular leaves and large, spurred flowers and can cover short fences and walls. Provide full sun and well-drained soils; water copiously when first planted. They are at their best in northern states, where summer temperatures remain cool. In Alaska or in the mountains, they can be spectacular.

Use cultivars with the word "climbing" in the description or name itself, such as 'Climbing Mixed'; otherwise, you will be disappointed.

'Moonlight' has soft yellow flowers on a 6- to 8-foot body.

'Spitfire' has flaming red flowers.

Tropaeolum peregrinum (per-i-gry'num)
canary creeper
annual

These may be more interesting than ornamental, but I think they are worth a try in the garden, if for no other reason than to have a few canaries flitting around. They produce pale green leaves that are generally deeply five-lobed. The odd canary-yellow flowers consist of two upper petals that are not only erect and large but are also cut, appearing to be fringed. The three lower petals are small and thin, making the upper ones look like the wings of canaries (so the story goes). They also bear a hooked green spur, making them even odder.

Plants are annuals and can be put out after the last frost, but they are still nasturtiums and decline as the weather heats up. They will be useless in most parts of the country by 1 July.

Propagation

Plants are propagated by seed. It is best to start them indoors, about two weeks before the last frost.

Method of climbing

Plants have twisting leaf stalks and can twine around thin structures.

Etymology

Tropaeolum, named by Linnaeus, from the Greek, *tropaion* ("trophy"), because when plants grew up a support, he was reminded of a classical trophy; *majus*, bigger, larger, for the flowers; *peregrinum*, exotic, for the unusual flowers. Nasturtium, Latin for a pungent-tasting plant.

Tropaeolum
peregrinum

Tropaeolum
peregrinum, habit.
Photo by Suzy Bales.

Vigna (vig′na)

Papilionaceae

Most of the species in the genus are used as green manures; some are culti-vated for the edible seeds and pods and added to soups and stews. One, *Vigna radiata*, mung bean, is best known in its young form as the popular bean sprout. Approximately 150 species are recognized, but only one is truly orna-mental, so let's try it.

Every now and then I come across articles with titles like "The Weirdest 10 Plants Ever," or "Plants Every Gardener Must See Before They Die"—with enough opinions and photos to immediately make one run out and find these unknown wonders of the world. I have never written such an article, but if I did, I might just include *Vigna caracalla*, snail vine. The name conjures up all sorts of images, but in fact, the image of a snail dangling from a vine is right on. Not only do you get a dangling snail, but a colorful and fragrant one at that. And they don't eat your hostas!

The three leaflets are ovate, hairy, and about 4 inches long and 3 inches wide. Plants will grow about 5 to 7 feet tall in most areas of the country, although if really happy, 15 feet has been noted, as has rampant growth in frost-free areas. Short axillary racemes of incredibly twisted and coiled flow-ers may occur in summer but generally not until mid fall. Buds occur in late summer, but patience is required as the buds take their sweet time open-ing. The flowers are about 2 inches long and usually open creamy white with

Vigna caracalla, habit

Vigna caracalla. Photo by Robert Bowden.

purple markings, which strengthen in color as they mature. The white turns to orange-yellow, and the purple gets darker. In its basic form, the flower is pea-shaped, having normal standard and keel petals, like those in hyacinth bean (*Lablab purpureus*) and scarlet runner bean (*Phaseolus coccineus*), but in this case, they are both elongated and the keel is twisted and coiled, resembling the shell of a snail or a corkscrew (corkscrew flower is its other common name). People's comments on the fragrance range from "barely noticeable" to "breathtaking" to "overwhelming." Plants are attractive to ants, which may be pollinators or simply attracted to the plant and flowers. Do not be concerned if a small army arrives one day; they are doing no harm. Beans occur inconsistently at best.

Plant in full sun or afternoon shade; fertilize consistently in the spring and early summer to help establish plants. Allow plants to climb a fence or short trellis.

Propagation
Plants are propagated by seed. It is best to start them indoors, about two weeks before the last frost.

Method of climbing
Plants have twisting leaf stalks and can twine and twist around small structures.

Etymology
Vigna, for Domenico Vigna (d. 1647), professor of botany at Pisa; *caracalla*, named for Caracas, Venezuela.

Vitis (vi′tis)
grape
Vitaceae

I suppose all grapes are ornamental, especially as the fruit forms and the imagining of the bountiful harvest begins. I guess the same could be said for tomatoes as well, so perhaps we need not get too carried away. However, to give grapes their due, even the wine grape, *Vitis vinifera*, has ornamental cultivars, such as 'Incana', with handsome white veins, and 'Purpurea', with deep purple foliage in the fall.

Others may argue that walking under an arbor of grape vines while admiring the dangling fruit makes one feel like Bacchus, and that grape vines are every bit as ornamental as a climbing rose or large-flowered clematis. If grapes are disease-free and can be grown in your area, then grow them.

And then invite me over to stroll beneath them so that I may revel in your bounty—and their beauty.

I am not sure if there is any consensus on an ornamental grape species, but probably the closest is the Japanese *Vitis coignetiae*, with a wonderful common name of crimson glory vine. This is a vigorous vine and can cover arbors, pergolas, and trees if allowed to do so. The rounded 4- to 5-inch-wide leaves are densely hairy beneath and can be showstoppers: dark green in the summer, turning a brilliant scarlet in the fall. The flowers and fruit are nothing to anticipate; the fruit is small, black, and scarcely edible. Plants are cold hardy to zone 5, but if grown with too much summer heat, they will have poor coloration. Of course, being a grape, they are susceptible to any number of fungi and hordes of Japanese beetles.

Another worth trying is the spiny grape, *Vitis davidii*. The stems are densely spined, and the new leaves are copper brown. They grow vigorously but take a few years to flower.

Vitis coignetiae

Propagation
Difficult. Try cuttings in the winter or late spring.

Method of climbing
Plants have tendrils from every third node which clasp upon structures or themselves.

Etymology
Vitis, the Latin name for the grapevine; *coignetiae*, unknown.

Vitis davidii,
new growth

Wisteria (wis-teer'ee-a)

Fabacaeae

These are vines you either love or hate—wisteria can beautify your garden, arbor, or wall or take over your entire town. Plants produce gnarled tree-like trunks and thousands of pendulous flowers in the spring and early summer. The compound leaves are alternate and slightly hairy on the undersides. I have seen plants climb to the top of 60-foot-tall trees, others espaliered against walls, and still others pruned to standards, growing like sentinels in large containers. Approximately ten species have been described, but two are most common in North American gardens.

Wisteria frutescens (frew-tes'enz)

American wisteria

zones 5–9

People did not embrace this native vine for many years because the racemes of flowers were shorter and the many flowers were closely arranged, giving the inflorescence a somewhat stubby appearance. Some claimed it did not have the elegance and grandeur of Japanese wisteria (*Wisteria floribunda*), from which dozens of cultivars have been developed. Hogwash. This is also a truly wonderful vine, native from Virginia to Florida and west to Texas. However, just because it is native, don't be fooled about its ability to grow. It may be a little slower than *W. floribunda* and *W. sinensis* (Chinese wisteria) but not

Wisteria frutescens. Photo
by Meg Green.

Wisteria frutescens
'Amethyst Falls'

so you would notice in the garden. It is still an exuberant grower and within five years will have covered whatever needed covering, including half your house. What it won't do is cover everyone else's house; it is not invasive.

Plants differ from Japanese and Chinese wisteria by flowering up to a month later; they also have significantly shorter racemes (only 5 to 6 inches) and usually fewer leaflets, and the standards often bear a yellow spot. They are not as fragrant and have been described as musky. I think the scent is terrific. Others have not been quite so kind, describing the scent thus: "like a male cat marked its territory on the shrub." Full sun.

'Alba' has white flowers.

'Amethyst Falls' is the most common cultivar and with good reason. It grows rapidly, bears flowers within two years of planting, and may even flower a second time. Fragrance is questionable.

'Magnifica' has lilac flowers with a more obvious yellow blotch on the standards.

Wisteria sinensis (si-nen′sis)
Chinese wisteria
zones 4–9

Goodness, when this plant is flowering all over the South in April, the sight and smell are glorious. The foliage consists of thirteen to nineteen leaflets, each one ovate to oblong and about 2 inches long. The lavender pea-like flowers occur in 10- to 15-inch-long axillary racemes, usually opening just as the leaves are reemerging in the spring. The flowers have the same form of other members of the family, with five petals including a large middle standard, two wings, and a keel made up of two fused petals beneath. Later in the summer, the long bean pods form.

It is truly one of the most beautiful vines I have seen, and it is easy to be enthralled and stare at the sight. Plants romp with abandon, and if you stare too long, it will romp over you. It is truly an invasive plant, and you are not doing any favors to your town by planting it without thinking. However, when properly pruned and trained on wires or over a long arbor, walking beneath the tresses of flowers is otherworldly. Use strong supports; this plant will tear down wooden structures. Prune ruthlessly by cutting about half the side stems back to about one half their length after flowering. Unfortunately, easier said than done.

If you are still planning on planting this vine, even after the words of warning, then enjoy the show. Plant in full sun and fertilize sparingly, or all you will get is foliage at the expense of flowers.

Wisteria sinensis. Photo by Alan Shapiro.

Propagation

Soak seeds of the species for twenty-four hours prior to sowing them. Germination is quite routine. Many cultivars are grafted, and cuttings of those will not perform with the same vigor as grafted individuals.

Method of climbing

Plants are twiners and twist around anything in their path. *Wisteria frutescens* and *W. floribunda* are said to twist in a clockwise pattern, *W. sinensis* counterclockwise, but I haven't seen that.

Etymology

Wisteria, for Caspar Wistar (1761–1818), professor of anatomy at the University of Pennsylvania; *floribunda*, many-flowered; *frutescens*, from the Latin *frutex* ("shrub'), normally referring to a shrubby habit but seems a misnomer here; *sinensis*, Chinese.

Wisteria sinensis, habit

Lists of Vines with Specific Characteristics and Uses

Annuals or biennials in zones 3–9

Perhaps cold hardy to zones 10/11. All could be included in conservatory/greenhouse culture. Generally grown as landscape/garden plants.

Adlumia	Cobaea	Lathyrus	Podranea
Allamanda	Cucurbita	Mandevilla	Psiguria
Asarina	Dalechampia	Manettia	Rhodochiton
Basella	Dioscorea	Mascagnia	Senecio
Berberidopsis	Eccremocarpus	Momordica	Solanum (most)
Canavalia	Gurania	Oxypetalum	Stictocardia
Cardiospermum	Ipomoea	Passiflora	Thunbergia
Cissus	Lablab	Petrea	Tropaeolum
Clitoria	Lagenaria	Phaseolus	Vigna

Cold hardy in zones 3–7

Not all species in listed genera are cold hardy. Zone shown is for most cold hardy species.

Aconitum (3)	Celastrus (4)	Hydrangea anomala ssp. petiolaris (4)	Rosa (many) (4/5)
Actinidia (4)	Clematis (many) (4)		Schizophragma (5)
Akebia (7)	Codonopsis (7)	Lonicera (5)	Solanum (7)
Ampelaster (7)	Decumaria (7)	Parthenocissus (4)	Trachelospermum (7)
Ampelopsis (4)	Dicentra (7)	Passiflora (7)	
Aristolochia (4)	Ficus (7)	Periploca (7)	Vitis (5)
Bignonia (7)	Gelsemium (7)	Polygonum (5)	Wisteria (4)
Campsis (4/5)	Hedera (5)		

Most often used for conservatory culure

All can be grown outdoors in summer but are seldom cold hardy in zone 7 or lower.

Allamanda	*Gurania*	*Podranea*
Antigonon	*Jasminum*	*Psiguria*
Aristolochia (most)	*Lathyrus*	*Quisqualis*
Berberidopsis	*Macfadyena*	*Rhodochiton*
Bougainvillea	*Mandevilla*	*Solanum* (most)
Cissus	*Manettia*	*Sollya*
Clerodendrum	*Pandorea*	*Tecomaria*
Clitoria	*Passiflora* (most)	*Vitis*
Dioscorea	*Petrea*	

Evergreen in zones 3–8

Most conservatory-grown specimens will remain evergreen.

Bignonia	*Decumaria*	*Hedera*
Clematis armandii	*Ficus*	*Lonicera* (some)
Clematis cirrhosa	*Gelsemium*	*Trachelospermum*

Small growers (under 10 feet)

Or all could easily be kept so with judicious pruning. All will attain more than 10 feet if perennialzed or if not pruned.

Aconitum	*Clematis* (some)	*Lonicera* (some)
Adlumia	*Cucurbita*	*Oxypetalum*
Akebia	*Eccremocarpus*	*Solanum*
Asarina	*Ficus*	*Sollya*
Berberidopsis	*Ipomoea*	*Thunbergia*
Cardiospermum	*Lathyrus*	*Tropaeolum*

Fragrance

All flowers are fragrant to someone. These are more obviously so.

Actinidia kolomikta	*Lonicera*	*Rosa*
Clematis armandii	*Mandevilla*	*Trachelospermum*
Gelsemium	*Pandorea*	*Vigna*
Jasminum	*Podranea*	*Wisteria*
Lathyrus		

Ornamental fruit

All plants (except sterile forms) produce fruit; the following genera produce conspicuous fruit.

Akebia	*Clitoria*	*Passiflora*
Campsis	*Cucurbita*	*Periploca*
Canavalia	*Lablab*	*Phaseolus*
Cardiospermum	*Lagenaria*	*Psiguria*
Celastrus	*Mascagnia*	*Rosa*
Clematis	*Momordica*	*Vitis*

Invasive reputation

Not all species within a genus are invasive. Some are invasive only in frost-free environments, others in temperate climes.

Akebia	*Dioscorea*	*Periploca*
Ampelopsis	*Hedera*	*Polygonum*
Campsis	*Ipomoea*	*Tecomaria*
Celastrus	*Lonicera*	*Trachelospermum*
Clematis	*Macfadyena*	*Wisteria*

Useful Conversions

INCHES	CENTIMETERS
$\frac{1}{3}$	0.8
$\frac{1}{2}$	1.25
1	2.5
$1\frac{1}{2}$	3.8
2	5.0
3	7.5
4	10
5	12.5
6	15
7	18
8	20
9	23
10	25
12	30
15	38
20	50
30	75
36	90

FEET	METERS
1	0.3
$1\frac{1}{2}$	0.5
2	0.6
$2\frac{1}{2}$	0.8
3	0.9
4	1.2
5	1.5
6	1.8
7	2.1
8	2.4
9	2.7
10	3.0
12	3.6
15	4.5
18	5.4
20	6.0
25	7.5
30	9.0
35	10.5
40	12
45	13.5
50	15
60	18

TEMPERATURES

$$°C = 5/9 \times (°F-32)$$
$$°F = (9/5 \times °C) + 32$$

Index of Botanical Names

Aconitum volubile, 14
Actinidia, 15
  arguta, 16
  deliciosa, 15
  kolomikta, 15, 16
  pilosula, 16
Adlumia fungosa, 18
Akebia, 19
  ×*pentaphylla*, 21
  quinata, 20
  trifoliata, 21
Allamanda, 21
  blanchetii, 22
  cathartica, 22
  neriifolia, 22
  schottii, 22
Ampelaster carolinianus, 24
Ampelopsis, 26, 57
  arborea, 27
  brevipedunculata, 26
Antigonon leptopus, 28
Aristolochia, 31
  clematitis, 31
  durior, 32
  gigantea, 34
  grandiflora, 11, 31, 34
  littoralis, 31
  macrophylla, 32
  sempervirens, 34
  tomentosa, 34
  trilobata, 34
Asarina, 35
  antirrhiniflora, 35, 36

  barclaiana, 35, 36
  lophospermum, 38
  procumbens, 35
  scandens, 38
Aster carolinianus, 22

Basella alba, 39
Basella rubra, 39
Berberidopsis corallina, 41
Bignonia capreolata, 42
Bougainvillea, 45
  glabra, 45
  spectabilis, 45

Calonyction aculeatum, 110
Campsis, 42, 48
  grandiflora, 48, 50
  radicans, 48, 50
  ×*tagliabuana*, 50
Canavalia, 52
  ensiformis, 53
  gladiata, 4, 5, 8, 52
Cardiospermum, 54
  grandiflorum, 55
  halicacabum, 54
Catalpa, 42
Celastrus, 55
  orbiculatus, 56
  scandens, 56
Cissus, 57
  amazonica, 57
  discolor, 57
  rhombifolia, 57
Clematis, 2, 4, 59

  alpina, 60
  armandii, 61
  cirrhosa, 62
  crispa, 73
  integrifolia, 77
  macropetala, 60
  montana, 60, 64
  reticulata, 77
  tangutica, 60, 68
  terniflora, 64, 69
  texensis, 60, 70
  viorna, 70
  viticella, 60
Clerodendrum, 79
  bungei, 79
  splendens, 79
  thompsoniae, 79
  trichotomum, 79
  ugandense, 79
Clitoria ternatea, 80
Cobaea scandens, 82
Codonopsis, 83
  clematidea, 84
  convolvulacea, 84
  ovata, 83
  tangshen, 84
Cucumis, 85
  melo, 85
  sativus, 85
Cucurbita, 85
  ficifolia, 85
  maxima, 85
  moschata, 85
  pepo, 85

Dalechampia dioscoreifolia, 87

Decumaria, 88, 106
  barbara, 88
  sinensis, 89
Dicentra scandens, 90
Dioscorea, 91, 180
  alata, 91
  bulbifera, 91
  cayenensis, 91
  rotunda, 91
Dipladenia, 136
Dolichos lablab, 125
Doxantha, 134

Eccremocarpus scaber, 93

Fallopia, 162
Ficus, 94
  benjamina, 94
  carica, 94
  elastica, 94
  pumila, 94

Gelsemium, 97
  rankinii, 98
  sempervirens, 97
Gurania malacophylla, 98, 164

Hedera, 100
  algeriensis, 105
  colchica, 101
  helix, 101, 102
Hoya, 146
Hydrangea, 82, 105, 176
  anomala, 105

Hydrangea [*continued*]
  petiolaris, 105

Ipomoea, 91, 108, 180
  alba, 108, 109
  batatas, 108, 110
  coccinea, 108, 121
  hederacea, 118
  lobata, 116
  nil, 118
  purpurea, 118
  quamoclit, 108, 121
  ×*sloteri*, 121
  tricolor, 108, 117

Jacaranda, 42
Jasminum, 122
  beesianum, 122
  nudiflorum, 122
  officinale, 122
  polyanthum, 122
  ×*stephanense*, 123

Lablab purpureus, 10, 125, 200
Lagenaria siceraria, 86
Lathyrus, 126
  latifolius, 126
  odoratus, 126, 127
  vernus, 126
Lobelia siphilitica, 80
Lonicera, 128
  ×*americana*, 129
  etrusca, 133
  ×*heckrottii*, 129, 130
  japonica, 129
  periclymenum, 132
  sempervirens, 129, 130
Lophospermum scandens, 38
Lythrum salicaria, 129

Macfadyena unguis-cati, 134

Mandevilla, 136
  ×*amabilis*, 136
  boliviensis, 136
  laxa, 136
  sanderi, 136
  splendens, 136
Manettia, 139
  cordifolia, 139
  luteorubra, 139
Mascagnia, 10, 141
  lilacina, 141
  macroptera, 141
Maurandya, 36
Maurandya anti-rrhiniflora.
  See *Asarina antirrhiniflora*
Mina, 116
Momordica charantia, 143

Nepeta, 16

Oxypetalum caeruleum, 146

Pandorea, 147
  jasminoides, 147
  pandorana, 148
Parthenocissus, 57, 149
  henryana, 151
  quinquefolia, 149
  tricuspidata, 150
Passiflora, 152
  alata, 155
  ×*alatocaerulea*, 154
  ×*allardii*, 155
  antioquiensis, 155
  ×*belotii*, 154
  biflora, 155
  boenderi, 152
  caerulea, 152
  coccinea, 153

  coriacea, 152, 153
  incarnata, 152
  ligularis, 152
  lutea, 152
  quadrangularis, 155
  racemosa, 155
Periploca, 157
  graeca, 157
  sepium, 157
Persicaria, 162
Petrea volubilis, 158
Phaseolus caracalla.
  See *Vigna caracalla*
Phaseolus coccineus, 159, 200
Podranea ricasoliana, 160
Polygonum, 162
  aubertii, 162
  baldschuanicum, 162
Pseudogynoxys chenopodioides, 178
Psiguria umbrosa, 164
Pueraria montana var. *lobata*, 134

Quisqualis indica, 165

Rehmannia, 160
Rhodochiton atrosanguineus, 167
Rosa, 6, 168
  banksiae, 171
  laevigata, 171
  multiflora, 169

Schizophragma, 82, 106, 176
  hydrangeoides, 176
  integrifolium, 2, 4, 176

Senecio confusus, 178
Solanum, 180
  crispum, 180
  dulcamara, 180
  jasminoides, 182
  mammosum, 80
  nigrum, 184
  wendlandii, 183
Sollya heterophylla, 185
Stephanandra, 14
Stictocardia, 186
  beraviensis, 187
  campanulata, 187

Tacsonia, 155
Tecoma, 42
Tecomaria capensis, 188
Thunbergia, 189
  alata, 189
  grandiflora, 191
  gregorii, 193
Trachelospermum, 193
  asiaticum, 194
  jasminoides, 193
Tropaeolum, 196
  majus, 197
  peregrinum, 13, 197
  speciosum, 196
  tuberosum, 196
Tweedia caerulea, 146

Vigna, 199
  caracalla, 199
  radiata, 199
Vitis, 57, 200
  coignetiae, 201
  davidii, 201
  vinifera, 200

Wisteria, 202
  floribunda, 202
  frutescens, 202
  sinensis, 203

Index of Common Names

air potato, 91, 180
allamanda, 22
    bush, 22
    purple, 22
Allegheny fleece vine,
    18

balloon vine, 54
balsam pear, 143
birthwort, 30, 35
bitter cucumber, 143
bittersweet, 10, 55
    American, 55
    oriental, 55
black-eyed Susan,
    189
bleeding heart, 18, 90
bleeding heart vine,
    79, 90
bluebell creeper, 185
blue pea, 80
Bolivian dipladenia,
    136
bonnet bellflower, 83
    climbing, 84
Boston ivy, 150
bougainvillea, 45
bow tie vine, 87
bower vine, 147
butterfly pea, 80
butterfly vine, 10, 141
    lilac, 141
    yellow, 141
butterfly weed, 146

calabash, 86
calico flower, 31

canary creeper, 197
Cape honeysuckle,
    188
cardinal climber, 121
cardinal flower, 108,
    121
Carolina jasmine, 97
catnip, 16
cat vine, 16
cat's claw, 134
Chilean glory flower,
    93
Chilean jasmine, 136
Chilean potato vine,
    180
Chinese foxglove, 160
Chinese gooseberry,
    15
chocolate vine, 19
clematis, 59
    anemone, 64
    Armand's, 61
    orange peel, 68
    sweet autumn, 69
    Texas, 70
    winter, 62
climbing aster, 24
climbing bleeding
    heart, 79, 90
climbing fig, 94
climbing fumitory,
    18
climbing hydrangea,
    88, 105, 176
climbing snap-
    dragon, 35
clock vine, 191

coral plant, 41
coral vine, 29
corkscrew flower,
    200
crimson glory vine,
    201
cross vine, 42
cucumber, 85
cup and saucer vine,
    82
cypress vine, 108,
    121

dang shen, 84
deadly nightshade,
    180
dinosaur gourd, 86
dipladenia, 136, 139
Dutchman's pipe, 33

everlasting pea, 126

fig, 94
firecracker plant, 139
fiveleaf akebia, 20
fleece vine, 162
foxglove, 160

ginseng, 84
glorybower, 79
    blue, 79
    harlequin, 79
    rose, 79
glorybower vine, 79
golden trumpet, 22
gourd, 85
    ball, 86

bottle, 86
egg, 86
orange-warted, 86
small spoon, 86
turban, 86
white-flowered, 86
grape, 26, 57, 200
gurania, 98, 164

Hawaiian sunset
    vine, 186
heartseed, 54, 55
honeysuckle, 128
    Cape, 128
    goldflame, 129
    Hall's, 130
    Japanese, 129
    trumpet, 130
hyacinth bean, 10,
    125, 200
hydrangea vine, 105
    Chinese, 176
    Japanese, 176

ivy, 100
    Algerian, 105
    Boston, 149
    English, 9, 10, 102
    Persian, 101

Jack bean, 4, 5, 8, 52
Japanese climbing
    hydrangea, 176
Japanese ivy, 150
jasmine, 122
Jerusalem cherry,
    180